YOU CAN DO THIS

YOU CAN DO THIS

Hope and Help for New Teachers

Robyn R. Jackson

JB JOSSEY-BASS™
A Wiley Brand

Published by Jossey-Bass
A Wiley Brand
One Montgomery Street, Suite 1200, San Francisco, CA 94104-4594—
www.josseybass.com

Jossey-Bass books and products are available through most bookstores. To
contact Jossey-Bass directly call our Customer Care Department within the U.S. at
800-956-7739, outside the U.S. at 317-572-3986, or fax 317-572-4002.

Wiley publishes in a variety of print and electronic formats and by print-on-demand.
Some material included with standard print versions of this book may not be included
in e-books or in print-on-demand. If this book refers to media such as a CD or DVD
that is not included in the version you purchased, you may download this material at
http://booksupport.wiley.com. For more information about Wiley products, visit
www.wiley.com.

Library of Congress Cataloging-in-Publication data is on file.
978-1-118-70205-5 (cloth) — 978-1-118-70197-3 (PDF) — 978-1-118-70209-3 (ePub)

Printed in the United States of America
FIRST EDITION
HB Printing   10 9 8 7 6 5 4 3 2 1

CONTENTS

To my parents—my first and best teachers

I didn't always want to be a teacher. For most of my childhood, I dreamed of being something way more sexy—a high-powered litigator or perhaps a glamorous fashion designer, maybe even an award-winning journalist. I wanted excitement and adventure, fame, and money and an interesting life. I thought I was dreaming big.

It wasn't until the spring of my senior year in high school that I realized that I was meant to be a teacher. I didn't have any lightning bolt from the heavens or a dramatic conversion moment. A teacher gave my class an assignment to research our future careers, and something inside me simply whispered, *you're going to be a teacher*.

So I researched the teaching profession and what I found wasn't very pretty. Basically, I was choosing a career that was a combination of very hard work and low pay. Although there was a modicum of respect for the work of teachers, it was not nearly as revered as a career in medicine, for example, or even business. It seemed as if I were taking a vow of poverty and obscurity. When I announced to my family and friends that I was going to major in education, they were supportive but some were mildly disappointed. "But you're so smart," some pointed out. "You could do so much better."

Nevertheless, when I started school, I approached my methods classes with real excitement. I eagerly gobbled up everything I was learning. I couldn't wait to start my student teaching and had an amazing experience with a masterful host teacher who showed me the tricks of the trade. I couldn't wait to have a classroom of my own.

When I finally did get my own classroom, I threw myself into my work. It was a struggle at first, but after some time, I found my way. A lot about teaching came naturally to me, and I loved my work. I also was lucky enough to meet some really masterful teachers who shared their knowledge with me. Every year, I got a little better. After a few years, I was asked to informally mentor a few teachers in my building and share with them some of the principles that made my teaching successful. Eventually I was requested to be an instructional coach in my school. I wasn't ready to leave the classroom yet, so I asked if I could be an instructional coach for half the day and teach the other half. During this time I taught three classes and spent the rest of the day helping other teachers become more effective.

When I first started coaching teachers, I simply told them the things that I did that were successful. I shared with them examples of interventions I was using with struggling students or told them how I set up my grading system. The problem was, while those strategies may have worked for me, they might not work for everyone. I had to stop and think about *why* those strategies worked for me. Soon, rather than share strategies, I started sharing *principles*, and that's when the teachers I coached really started to see a difference in their practice. Rather than tell them how I set up interventions, for instance, I showed them the principle of proactive interventions, where teachers intervene early, before a student gets into a free fall of failure, and then showed them how to set up intervention systems on their own. What was surprising to me was how any teacher could take the principles I shared and make them work, no matter which students or which subjects they taught. I loved seeing how teachers would take the principles I shared with them and make them their own. I'd go into their classrooms and instead of seeing a carbon copy of my class, I'd see that they had used the principles to create a classroom and a teaching style that worked for them. The principles were the same, but their classrooms looked like them, not like me.

After some time, I was recruited to become an administrator at a different school. Being an administrator was a tougher transition than I thought it would be, because I still had a coaching mindset and now I was being asked to evaluate other teachers. I didn't understand the change in the power dynamic, and so it took a few adjustments on my part.

Eventually I learned how to provide feedback during evaluations so that the process was supportive and useful to teachers. Again, I kept the focus on principles rather than techniques so that teachers could take my feedback and use it in a way that was specific to their needs, their students' needs, and their own teaching styles.

After a few years as an administrator, I was offered a promotion within the district. After some soul searching, I turned it down, quit my job, and started writing my first book, *Never Work Harder Than Your Students*, to share the principles I had been learning and teaching throughout my career with other teachers. While I was writing that book, I started my company, Mindsteps, with the idea that any teacher could become a master teacher with the right kind of support and practice, and started helping thousands of teachers learn these principles and apply them to their practices.

I went on to write eight more books and help a lot of teachers use these principles to make the difference they wanted to make in their classrooms, but something troubled me. Many teachers had become so frustrated over the years that they had lost touch with their own passion and lost sight of their own reasons for becoming teachers in the first place.

I thought back to my own early years of teaching and how much I love this profession. From the moment I realized that

> *...a lot of what you learn in the first few years of teaching sets you up for unrealistic expectations...*

I was meant to become a teacher until today, I have believed that this is the most amazing, interesting, challenging, important work that anyone can do. I know that many teachers enter this profession holding this same belief. What happens, I wondered, that erodes that belief over time?

I have given this a great deal of thought, and now I am convinced that a lot of what we learn in the first few years of teaching sets you up for unrealistic expectations of what this amazing profession is and what role we play in it. We are taught early on to conform, to answer to mandates and dictums, and to play it safe. Rather than feed our own passion and awaken a passion for learning in others, we can get distracted by test scores or disheartened by the very real challenges that we face every day. It can get really easy to lose sight of why we are here and the difference we came to this profession to make.

This book has been on my heart for several years now. I even tried to write it once before but couldn't quite find the words. New teachers often approach me with the challenges of their classrooms and want me to give them advice. *What should I do about this?* or *How can I manage that?* they ask me. I look into their expectant eyes and I know what they want. They want me—the author, keynote speaker, and consultant—to tell them what to do, to share some bit of sage wisdom that will make everything turn out okay. What I knew, and what kept me from writing this book for a long time, was that I can't.

That's the thing about teaching. What worked for me or for other teachers I have worked with may not work for you. I cannot solve your teaching challenges for you. I don't have a magic formula that will make teaching easy or erase every pitfall that awaits you. Even if I could, I wouldn't, because I firmly believe that what will make you a master teacher is not the advice I give you; what will make you a master teacher is that you figure out how to solve those challenges on your own, your own way.

That's why I wrote this book. Not to give you advice— although I do share some advice I've learned along the way. The reason I wrote this book is to help you figure it out on your own. I share stories from my own experience, not so that you can emulate my path, but so you can find your own path. The rules of teaching, the ones that you learned in school or that have been touted by some education consultant (me included), or those practices that are embraced without question by your school system, may not be the right rules for you. You can learn from my experiences, but ultimately what I hope you learn is how to find your own way.

And for me, that's the secret to surviving your first years of teaching. You have to find your own path, your own teaching style, your own way.

But don't worry.

You can do this.

My first year of teaching was almost twenty years ago, and yet I still vividly remember what it felt like to finally have a classroom of my own and do what I believe I was put on this earth to do—teach. However, I could not have become the teacher I am today without the help of some very masterful teachers along the way—Talia Shaw, Helen Marshall, Marjorie Richardson, Esther Mattox, Flora Kellogg, Todd Nelson, Sylvia Barnes, Bernard Benn, Ramona Hyman, Derek Bowe, Jan Dulan, Barbara Bass, and Mary Helen Washington. Nor could I have learned to teach with mastery without those teachers who mentored me in my early years. Thank you, Tom Gillard, Erika Huck, and Cynthia Gill, for taking me under your wings and showing me how to be a great teacher.

This book could never have happened without the persistence and patience of my editor, Marjorie McAneny. Thank you for helping me develop the idea for this book and for your patience with me as I wrote it. It has been a real pleasure working with you.

At Mindsteps, I am blessed to be surrounded with other teachers who continually refine my practice. Thank you, Valda, Linda, Christine, Beverly, John, Sheri, and JoJo.

One of the things I love the most about what I do is that I get to work with exceptional educators all over the world. Thank you to everyone who has taken time to share a tip in a comment on our blog, or stayed behind to talk with me after a speech, or taken a risk and tried something new during a workshop, or exchanged e-mails with me in the Mindsteps Vault, or bravely opened up your classroom and let me be a part of your journey toward mastery. It is an honor and a privilege to serve you. It is because of you that I continue to learn and grow toward mastery.

I want to especially thank those of you who are just starting out on this journey. You've chosen the best of professions. I am inspired by your bravery and your passion, and I am awed by the work you do.

Finally, I would not be who I am or do what I do without the support of those who love me the most. I am immeasurably blessed to have a mom, dad, and sister who love me just as I am. If that weren't blessing enough, I also get to bask in the love and support of a man like Charles. Believe me; they make all the difference.

ROBYN R. JACKSON, PHD, is passionate about the teaching profession. A former high school English teacher and middle school administrator, she is founder and president of Mindsteps, Inc., a Washington, DC–based provider of professional development for teachers and administrators.

Robyn is the author of nine previous books, including the bestselling *Never Work Harder Than Your Students & Other Principles of Great Teaching* (ASCD, 2009) and the Mastering the Principles of Great Teaching series (ASCD). Through her speaking and training, she inspires audiences worldwide to become master teachers, implement more rigorous instruction, support struggling students, and provide effective instructional leadership.

To learn more, go to www.mindstepsinc.com.

YOU CAN DO THIS

CHAPTER 1

YOU CAN BE YOURSELF

DEVELOPING YOUR OWN TEACHING STYLE

When I first started teaching, I wanted to be a combination of all the movie and television teachers I'd seen over the years. I wanted to be noble and inspirational like Sidney Poitier in *To Sir with Love*. I wanted the steely determination of Jaime Escalante in *Stand and Deliver*. I wanted the combined toughness of Joe Clark in *Lean on Me* and Debbie Allen of *Fame*. I wanted the unconventionality of Michelle Pfeiffer in *Dangerous Minds*. And I wanted the lovable, goofy sense of humor of Gabe Kaplan in *Welcome Back Kotter*. I thought the combination would make me a master teacher.

So I went to work each day trying to shape myself into the image of my ideal teacher. I planned quirky lessons in the name of being innovative. I created unreasonable requirements in the name of being tough. Because I taught high school and looked younger than most of my students,

I dressed like an old school marm—sensible heels, skirts that came almost to my ankles, frumpy blouses, and glasses. My sister started calling me Miss Crabtree.

I wanted to make a difference, so I threw myself into my teaching. I applied all the theories I had learned in my methods classes. I wrote lesson plans every day and spent every weekend grading papers. I faithfully followed the curriculum. I posted and enforced classroom rules. I created elaborate differentiated lessons designed to tap into each student's learning style and multiple intelligences. I used technology. I collaborated with my colleagues. I applied cooperative instruction, inquiry-based learning, multiculturalism—you name it. In short, I tried to become my idea of the perfect teacher.

Soon, however, I realized that there was a stark difference between my ideal classroom and the one I was actually running. That assignment I spent hours planning fell flat. That really cool strategy I couldn't wait to try failed to engage my students. At first, I thought it was just a matter of accumulating newer strategies, better lessons, different approaches. So I devoted myself to learning as much as I could. I read the "happy teacher" books that made teaching seem so easy. I watched master teachers smoothly handle their students. I developed a great grasp of the facts of teaching and worked harder and harder until I burned myself out. But despite all this hard work, some of my students were still disengaged, bored, and barely learning.

For a while, I even blamed my students. They were lazy. They didn't care. Their parents were bad parents. Sometimes the blame even came in the form

> *My dreams about the kind of teacher I would be were more about serving my own ego needs than serving my students.*

of more acceptable excuses—they were too impacted by poverty, they had really short attention spans because of so much television and social media, this generation just doesn't have the same values—but the bottom line was that I was not as effective with them as I dreamed I would be.

It took me a long time and a lot of frustration before I understood that the problem wasn't my students. The problem was my *approach* to my students. I realized over time that my dreams about the kind of teacher I would be were more about serving my own ego needs than serving my students. I wanted my students to do well because that would mean that I was a good teacher. I wanted them to tearfully thank me at the end of the year and tell me how much I had changed their lives. I wanted to recount stories of the difference I had made in the lives of my students to my awestruck friends at the next dinner party. I wanted my students to grow up, become famous, and thank me in their Nobel Prize acceptance speeches. I wanted someone to make a movie about *me*. In fact, many of my dreams about teaching weren't about helping my students at all. They were about me.

Once I came to that very painful (and a little embarrassing) realization, I shifted my focus away from me and my own twisted ideals to my students. I stopped trying to manipulate them to learn and showed them *how* to learn. I stopped trying to get my students to serve my own ego needs and started serving theirs.

The difference was almost immediate and so radical that I never turned back. For the first time in my teaching career, I felt free. In trying to become my idea of a master teacher, I had failed miserably. Once I shed those ideas, focused instead on my students and their needs, and relaxed, I was able to just teach. As a result, over time I become the very kind of teacher I'd always dreamed I would be.

You wouldn't be able to make a compelling movie about the changes that happened in my classroom. There were days when my lessons soared, and other days when they tanked. There were days when my students loved me and days when I just got on their nerves and vice versa. But by simply focusing on teaching well rather than focusing on becoming the perfect teacher, I found my own teaching style, my own version of mastery, and I promise you that you can too. Here's how.

GO AHEAD AND BORROW A FEW TRICKS, BUT REMEMBER WHO YOU ARE

I don't know about you, but when I first started teaching, I felt a lot of pressure to have a "bag of tricks." I copied every exciting lesson I found, and I visited other teachers' classrooms and "stole" their handouts, activities, even their bulletin board ideas. I kept files and notebooks of cool things I had seen others do. Whenever I planned a new lesson, I would reach into my bag of tricks and pull out someone else's strategy, someone else's lesson, and try to make it work in my classroom. Sometimes I succeeded. Most of the time, however, I was barely able to pull it off.

At first I felt like a bad teacher. After all, other teachers had used this lesson or that worksheet successfully. Why couldn't I? It wasn't until much later in the year that I realized the problem: I was trying to make other people's lessons work without really understanding why they chose this material or that strategy. I was trying to shoehorn myself into other teachers' lesson plans instead of figuring out

> *I was trying to shoehorn myself into other teacher's lesson plans instead of figuring out whether their lessons would work for my students and my teaching style.*

whether their lessons would work for my students, my teaching style, and my learning objectives for my students.

It's okay to take ideas from other teachers. We all do it. But you must always keep in mind who you are, who your students are, and what you want to accomplish with your students before you choose to use another's idea with your class. What works for one teacher may not work for you. What makes sense in one classroom may not be a good fit for yours. So go ahead and beg, borrow, or steal, but do so with discretion. Take time to examine why the lesson worked so that you can adapt it for your purposes later on.

LEARN FROM OTHERS, BUT DO WHAT WORKS FOR YOU

When I first started teaching, I did things the way that others showed me because I didn't know any better. While I learned a lot, some of the systems I'd been taught didn't work for me. I found them clunky or cumbersome. Although those systems worked for the teachers who showed them to me, I needed something more efficient.

For instance, each marking period, several teachers in my department used to issue "incompletes" to any student who was missing an assignment. They did it because they felt it would help students to turn in their work. Once report cards were issued, students had ten days to turn in any missing work or their "incomplete" grade turned into a failing grade.

Because this was the way that things were done, I followed along. But soon, I began to question this policy. It just didn't make sense to me. Most students turned in the missing work but they copied it from other students or rushed through it. I hardly graded it, just slashing off 50 percent (according to the late work policy at the time) and recorded the grade in my gradebook. Those students who were failing either didn't turn in the work because they were going to fail anyway, or worse, did turn in the work in hopes of not failing and still failed. Students thought the policy was a joke, and soon, so did I.

And yet, two more marking periods came and went without my saying anything. Finally, I mentioned to another teacher that I thought the policy did little to prevent missing assignments, and he secretly agreed with me. We decided that we weren't going to do it anymore and went to our department chair to discuss it. She strenuously protested, but since the policy was not a district one, she couldn't force us to comply.

The next marking period was a revelation. I didn't have any more missing work than I normally had. But my students and I

Don't accept every informal policy as gospel. Figure out what works best for you and your students.

weren't stressed out at the end of the marking period. Instead, I worked with them throughout the quarter to get their work in on time, and by the end of the year, I had developed a late work policy my students and I could live with.

It's easy to just do what everyone else is doing when you first start teaching. But don't accept every informal policy as gospel. Figure out what works best for you and your students.

TAKE TIME TO REFLECT   I know, I know. You don't *have* any time. Yes, I get it. But this one is important. It is the only way I know for you to become your best quickly. In fact, this is the secret to much of my teaching success over the years.

Early in my teaching career, the pressures of state tests, earning tenure, and just making it through the day in one piece were taking their toll on me. I had fantasized for so long about having my own classroom and teaching my own way, and yet I felt trapped by the demands of my job. Teaching just wasn't as fun as I'd hoped it would be.

I shared my concern with a trusted colleague, and she assured me that it would get better. I asked her when it got better for her. Her answer? Three years.

Three years? I wasn't going to make it three years. I was working my butt off trying to twist myself into what I thought was a master teacher, and I was weary. The summer after my first year of teaching, I decided to take a course on teaching writing through the Maryland Writing Project. It was an intense summer, but what I learned in that course saved me. The first day we arrived, we were asked to write for half an hour about whatever came to mind. In fact, we spent much of our time over the six weeks writing, reflecting, and thinking about our teaching. It wasn't all we did, but it was a huge part of the process, and it was transformative to my teaching. During that six-week period, away from the noise and pressures of teaching, I reconnected with who I wanted to be as a teacher, what my goals were, and what difference I wanted to make for my students. Doing so reignited my passion, and I swore I would never let that flame go out again. I thought about what worked, what didn't work, what I needed, and what my students needed to be successful. I paid attention to my own teacher voice, and started right then to construct my own teacher self.

Since that summer, I have never been the same. Simply taking time to reflect helped me listen to my own voice and make sense of my own teaching. Although I never had a solid six weeks again for that kind of learning and reflection, I have found that, sometimes, I just need a quiet hour over the weekend, or a morning during a school holiday, to take time and think. Sometimes, I have even gotten up thirty minutes earlier (and I am no morning person, trust me!) and spent time reflecting before a particularly stressful day ahead. Even today, when I start to get over-whelmed with all that I want to accomplish, I take time to reflect. It is my number one way to figure out my own teaching practice, make dramatic leaps in my expertise, and develop new and better ways to do what I do.

YOU'RE ALLOWED TO EXPERIMENT   When you first start teaching, you want to do everything per-fectly. We all do. We're so afraid to make a mistake or do some-thing wrong that we stick to the book. But you'll never figure out

> *The only way to find out what works for you is to try a lot of ideas until you find the ones that fit.*

your own teaching mojo if you do. The only way to find out what works for you is to try a lot of ideas until you find the ones that fit.

Once I started experimenting, I was able to find my own way. In fact, some of my best teaching ideas started as experiments in the classroom. Even today, experimenting is the way that I develop new and better teaching strategies as a consultant. Along the way, I've learned a few lessons on how to experiment successfully:

1. **Always start with a problem you are trying to solve**. There is no point to experimenting for experimenting's

sake. Instead, root any experiment in a problem. That way, you'll know whether your experiment was successful by whether it resolved the problem.

2. **Focus on the root cause**. Once you identify the problem you want to solve, try to figure out what the root cause of the problem is rather than get distracted by some of its symptoms. For instance, my students weren't responding to the comments on their papers and improving from one paper to the next. It would have been easy to think that they weren't responding simply because they were being lazy, but that would have been a superficial analysis on my part. The real reason they weren't responding to my comments was that they didn't know how. Once I realized that was the root cause, I could come up with a solution that would really make a difference. If you are unsure of the root cause, spend some time reflecting on your challenge either in writing or with a trusted colleague. Alternatively, ask your students to tell you what they think the real problem is.

3. **Do your research first**. Now that you understand the root cause, look around to see if anyone has already come up with a solution. Check with your colleagues, online, and in books, or visit the educational research. Perhaps you can alter something you find or use something you find as a catalyst for creating your own solution.

4. **Try something and see whether it works**. Now you're ready to experiment, but your experiment is more likely to yield fruit because you have thought things through ahead of time.

5. **Reflect**. After your experiment, think about not only the effect if had on your students but how it felt to you as well. Were you comfortable? Did it fit in with your emerging teaching style? Did it feel right? Do you need to tweak it somehow? Reflect either alone or with a mentor or other trusted colleague and record your thoughts.

6. **Make adjustments and try it again**. Once you've taken time to think things through, tweak the parts that didn't quite work, throw out the parts that utterly failed, and save the best parts to combine with other teaching strategies or use on their own. Then, as soon as you can, try it again and repeat the process until you have something that works for you.

So go ahead. Experiment. You won't break anything. Sometimes your experiment will be a smashing success. Other times it will be an abject failure. That's okay. That's how you figure out what works for you and your students. The beauty of teaching is that if your experiment fails, there is always tomorrow. You can try again.

I know everything feels a little awkward right now, but trust me: You will develop your own teaching style over time if you commit to being yourself. I know that you are probably feeling pressure to immediately morph into a master teacher. I know that you have an idea in your head about how you *should* teach, *should* behave, and the amazing results you *should* have. What's more, you are probably getting pressure from the outside (colleagues, supervisors, mentors, parents, and even your students) to be perfect right away. But mastery takes time. This awkward stage you are going through right now is absolutely necessary if you ever hope to become a master teacher. In fact, it is critical. It is the only way that you are going to figure out your own teaching style and what works for you.

Finding your own teaching style is the right work to be doing right now. You can never be as good at being someone else as you can at being yourself. The good news is that mastery isn't dependent on having a certain personality or doing things a certain way. Mastery isn't based on a prescribed list of behaviors. It's based on a simple set of principles, and as such, it can and will look different for each person or personality who applies them. That means that you can be yourself and still be masterful. In fact, it means that you absolutely should.

CHAPTER 2

YOU CAN HAVE A LIFE
FINDING BALANCE

My first year of teaching is in many ways a blur. It was challenging and exhilarating, yes, but mostly I remember it being downright exhausting. I'd get up at 5:30 each morning and leave my house by 6:15, and drive up to an hour in morning rush hour traffic to arrive at school and start my first period at 7:25. School finished at 2:00, but I didn't leave the building until 3:30, only to drive an hour home in rush hour traffic, spend another hour or two grading, eat dinner, iron whatever I was wearing to work the next day, shower, and fall into bed exhausted by 9:00 pm. I spent Saturday night and most of the day Sunday grading and planning and just trying to keep my head above water.

The hardest part was that I couldn't stop thinking about my kids. I even dreamed about school. It seemed that during the week and much of the weekends I was always planning instruction, delivering instruction, or grading. No television, no fun nights out with friends, no long talks on the phone, no dates. I just worked.

I meet a lot of new teachers who are just as dedicated as I was. They have the same passion and commitment to their students. They, too, want to be really good at teaching, and that desire drives them to eat, drink, and sleep their jobs. However, you *can* have a life as a new teacher. You can find a way to balance the very real demands of teaching with the equally real need to have a life outside of teaching. Here's what I've learned.

START WITH THE LITTLE MOMENTS

I started teaching after I had earned my master's degree. The first six months of my teaching career, I did nothing but teach. After that, I enrolled in a full-time doctoral program while I taught. Juggling the two was pretty difficult at first. I'd work all day and then rush to class in the evenings. Sometimes I wouldn't get out of class until 10:00 pm, and I had to be at work at 7:00 am the next morning (after an hour commute). In my free time, I was studying or writing papers. I didn't have a lot of money, so I was trying to get through school as quickly and efficiently as possible.

Soon, my days began to bleed together. I was exhausted all the time and struggled to maintain my focus on any one thing. I never saw my friends, I never read for pleasure any more, I didn't watch television or go out. All I did during the week was work, study, eat, and sleep (and I rarely slept). I was twenty-five, but I felt like I was one hundred years old. I looked like I was about that old too.

One day, my mother called, and as we talked, she said, "Honey, I am concerned about you. All you do is work and go to school. What about a life?"

"What life?" I snorted. "I don't have time for a life."

"Well, you need to make time," she warned. "There's more to life than work, you know. I worry about you."

At first I dismissed her concern. After all, she's a mom and she's supposed to worry. Besides, I thought she had no idea how hard it was to juggle all that I had on my plate. Over the next few days, however, my weekday routine of work, school, eat, sleep began to chafe. I started to see that it wasn't very much of a life. I began to miss the things I used to do.

Around that time, a friend of mine recommended a new novel for me to read and gave me his copy. I badly wanted to read that novel; it had been so long since I'd read anything but journal articles and textbooks. But where, I wondered, would I find the time?

I mentioned my dilemma to another friend, and she suggested that my problem was that I was trying to read the whole novel at one sitting, as I was used to

One page a night does not a life make. But it was a breakthrough for me.

doing. Instead, I could read it a little at a time. So I made a promise to myself that no matter what else was going on, I would read at least one page from the novel every night before going to bed.

Now that might seem trivial to you. One page a night does not a life make. But it was a breakthrough for me. I remember that some nights I found time to read several pages, even an entire chapter. Other nights, it was all I could do to keep my eyes open long enough to get through that page. It wasn't my preferred way of reading, but keeping that commitment to myself, to take at least a few minutes each day and do something that had nothing to do with work, school, eating, or sleeping showed me that I could and should carve out time for myself, even if that time was nothing more than a few stolen moments to read one page from a novel.

I started thinking about other things I used to enjoy that I didn't do any more. I made a concerted effort to find a few moments each day for those simple pleasures: Kneading dough for homemade bread soothed me; spending time with my godchildren buoyed my spirits; a stolen few moments for a phone call to a friend kept me con-

When I started focusing on those few moments here or there rather than waiting for a big chunk of time, I was able, at last, to cobble together a life.

nected. When I started focusing on those few moments here or there rather than waiting for a big chunk of time, I was able, at last, to cobble together a life.

OBSERVE A "SABBATH"

There is a natural rhythm to life of activity and rest. If you fail to honor that rhythm, you pay the consequences in terms of your health, your stress level, and your productivity. It may seem counterintuitive, but taking time off actually helps you to be *more* productive in the long run.

I grew up observing Sabbath from sunset Friday to sunset Saturday. During that time my family and I refrained from all work and anything secular. Instead, we spent time reconnecting with family and close friends, worshiping at church, and resting. When I started teaching and, shortly thereafter, enrolled in a doctoral program, I still observed Sabbath no matter how busy I was, and I never once regretted it.

I remember being given take-home exams to complete over the weekend. My friends at school thought I was crazy to sacrifice a precious day of my weekend not working on the exam, especially when it came to my comprehensive exams, which determined whether I would be able to remain in the program or progress on to the next stage. But I worked on those exams Friday after work until sunset and then put them away. I didn't even allow myself to think about them until the sun set on Saturday evening. Then I would take the exam out and finish it by the Sunday or Monday deadline. Taking this time off made my performance on those exams so much more focused. I never once did poorly on an exam by taking the time over the weekend to rest.

Although I observe Sabbath every week because of religious reasons, I have friends who observe secular Sabbaths as well. One friend takes a "cyber-sabbath" every Saturday; she shuts down all her devices and spends the day with her two children. Another friend "unplugs" each Sunday, ignoring her phone, e-mail, and computer for the day to spend time alone thinking, reflecting, taking long walks outside, and rejuvenating in preparation for her week. Still another friend takes each Friday afternoon to rest, go for a walk, see a movie, or read a book for pleasure—anything but work. I know others who take Sunday mornings or Wednesday afternoons or one weekend per month to take a step back, rest, and rejuvenate. Pick something that works with your schedule, your priorities, and your lifestyle, but please, take the time.

Resting, taking time to relax, is the secret to a happy and productive life. I know that you are busy and overwhelmed. It may seem at times that you will never get caught up. Your house is a mess and your bills haven't been paid in weeks and you really need to run a few errands. Remember that you also need time to rest, to get away from it all, and to take time for yourself. To this day, I observe a weekly Sabbath. Not matter how messy my house is, no matter what errands need to be run or what bills need to be paid, or even what other important tasks I've been putting off, when the sun sets on Friday, I turn it all off and focus on the things that are deeply important to me. I spend the time resting. It—whatever it is—will still be there on Saturday night, and because I have taken the time to rest, I am more equipped to handle it.

FIND WAYS TO BE MORE EFFICIENT

Because everything is new, it's hard to figure out how to be more efficient. Besides, you want to do a good job, so you're likely to be very thorough. However, you need to look for ways to streamline your work so that you don't become overwhelmed. I know that when I first started teaching, I couldn't figure out how to get it all done during the day. Yet, I'd see other teachers who managed to keep up with the grading and planning and still have hobbies, families, and interesting, full lives outside of work. I knew that it could be done. I just needed to figure out how.

So I started asking around. How do you keep up with attendance? What do you do about late work? How do you handle parent e-mails? May I take a look at your filing system? And those amazing veteran teachers were happy to share with me their secrets.

One showed me the trick of never taking paperwork to her desk. Instead, she took her gradebook down to the main office once per day and filled out all the 504s, IEPs, and counselor and coach requests waiting in her box right there in the main office. That way, she got through the paperwork quickly and never lost a single paper. Another teacher showed me how to organize my files not alphabetically, but by units, so that the proper documents were all together. It saved me a ton of time and kept me much more organized. Yet another teacher showed me a better way to organize my grades and a system for weighting grades that made much more sense and was much fairer than the system I was using. Not everything everyone shared worked for me, but after a month of really trying to get systems in place, I had a set of processes that made me much more efficient. And I constantly tweaked them over the first few years of teaching, until I had things running smoothly in a way that worked best for me.

Early on, create systems and processes for every part of your job. Ask the veterans in your building to share their systems rather than reinventing the wheel yourself. And tweak and customize what you learn until it works for you. The more efficient you are, the more of a life you can have outside of school.

ONLY GIVE MEANINGFUL WORK

One of the things that helped me the most was taking stock of what I was doing and what things were taking up most of my time. I taught writing and believed that my students should write as much as possible, so I assigned them an essay to write each week. I thought that the practice would make them better writers. The problem was that every Friday, I would collect those essays and promptly ruin my weekend. Either I'd spend all weekend grading the essays so that I could have them back to the students by Monday, or all weekend I'd feel guilty about not getting through those essays, and then spend Monday frantically trying to catch up. Either way, the quality of my feedback was poor because I was rushing, and the quality of their essays didn't improve because my students didn't have enough time between assignments to work on the feedback and improve their own writing.

I also assigned homework every night like I thought that a good teacher should. Again, more grading for me and, because I was often assigning homework just for the sake of giving homework, the quality of my students' work deteriorated as they focused more on getting the work in and jumping through my homework hoops than actually working through my assignments meaningfully.

But there were small ways that I was inefficient too. Because I was only a few days ahead of my students in terms of my planning, I made copies almost every day. I didn't have systems in place to make the class run smoothly, so I wasted a lot of time doing things like organizing books to distribute or collect, figuring out where to put things, and organizing papers to return. I needed a better way.

The first thing I did was streamline my assignments. Tom, a wise teacher who taught next door to me, stopped by my classroom one day and looked at the piles of papers all over my desk and asked,

"What's all this?"

"Homework I have to grade." I leaned back, closed my eyes, and rubbed my temples. "If I die young, it will probably be because I've been buried by an avalanche of student papers," I lamented dramatically.

Tom smiled. "Why don't you stop giving so much homework?"

My eyes shot open. Tom was speaking blasphemy. "But I have to give homework," I sputtered incredulously. "How else will my students learn?"

"I didn't say *never* give homework," Tom rolled his eyes. "But do you have to give it every night? I mean, come on," he said picking up a set of poorly constructed vocabulary sentences from a stack of student papers. "Do you really think your students will suffer because they didn't have to go home tonight and write ten more awkward sentences using the word 'persevere'?"

"They need the practice," I said defensively as I tried to take the paper back from Tom.

"What are they really practicing?" Tom asked. I sat there and stared at him. I really didn't know.

"But don't we *have* to give them homework?" I asked.

"When they need it," Tom said as he handed my student's paper back to me and headed to the door. He paused at the door and looked at me meaningfully as he reached for the knob. "But only when they need it."

I watched Tom leave, and to be honest, my first thought was that he wasn't as good a teacher as I thought he was. I mean, how could he not require homework? But over the next few days as I paid attention to the homework I assigned and collected from my students, Tom's advice began to make more sense. I really was assigning too much homework, and it wasn't making a huge difference in my students' writing. So I experimented, and for a week, instead of giving homework every night, I only assigned homework when I thought my kids needed it. Instead of hurting my students, they actually began to take the homework I did assign much more seriously. I got *more* homework from the students, not less.

> *I only assigned homework when I thought my kids needed it. I got* more *homework from the students, not less.*

So I stopped giving homework every night. I also took a look at what else I was doing. I stopped assigning an essay per week. I stopped giving assignments just for the sake of giving assignments and tried to ensure that whatever I did assign was meaningful.

My students didn't suffer. In fact, more of them turned in their homework on time and made more progress because the homework I did assign was more meaningful. What's more, I did a better job of returning their work quickly because there was less to grade. My students got the feedback they needed to improve their performance. Less really was more in this case.

Letting go of the dogma that I had to give homework every night freed me to give my students homework that actually counted. The same principle is true about most assignments. Don't give work for the sake of giving work. It wastes both your time and your students' time. Instead, make sure that the work you give is meaningful. That way, completing it and grading it will be time well spent.

DON'T TRY TO DO IT ALL

I first met Karen when I was doing instructional coaching at her school. Like many new teachers, she was trying to do it all. Karen wanted so badly to be a good teacher, but quite frankly, she put so much pressure on herself that by December, she was completely overwhelmed. One day while working with me on developing a rigorous learning unit, she broke down crying.

"Why are you crying?" I asked, concerned.

"I'm sorry," she sniffed as she wiped her eyes. "I'm so sorry. It's just that I am so overwhelmed. I work and work and work, and no matter how hard I try, it's never enough. I'm under all this pressure to get my test scores up, and I am still learning the ropes."

I handed her a tissue. "Karen," I began gently. "What you need is a stop doing list."

"A stop doing list?" she asked, puzzled. "I don't understand."

"Well, as teachers we are very good at creating 'to do' lists," I explained. "We end up adding more and more things to our list and becoming more and more overwhelmed. Let's take some time to clear some space in your day so that you can focus on the things that are really important."

From there, I asked Karen to list all the things she did that day. Then we went back through her list and divided every activity into one of four categories: time wasters, time consumers, empowerment failures, and finally the Important.

The time wasters, such as working on ineffective warm-up activities, getting into pointless arguments with students, and grading certain practice assignments, we immediately *eliminated*.

The time consumers we found ways to *automate*. For instance, Karen was required by her district to keep a professional portfolio. She spent hours each week adding material to her portfolio. I suggested that she streamline the process and organizer her portfolios while sitting in faculty meetings during the housekeeping items that didn't concern her. She could put it away when the meeting demanded more of her attention. Karen also was required to provide additional support for struggling students. I shared with her how to create a proactive support plan as a way to automate many of the support practices that were eating away at her time.

For the empowerment failures, we *delegated* to students or other adults in the building. We found that Karen had a lot of empowerment failures. Like many well-intentioned teachers, she was trying to fill all the gaps in the building—taking on extra duties outside of her area of responsibility because no one else on her team seemed to be stepping up. As a result, she was burning herself out. So we identified areas she needed to delegate to other members of her team. Then we looked for areas where *she* was doing all the work, not her students, and worked on strategies to give the work back to her students.

Finally, we looked at what was left and discussed why it was important. Karen immediately began to relax as she talked about how much she loved helping students discover their own voice through her teaching process. However, with all of the time wasters, time consumers, and empowerment failures in the way, she rarely had time to do the things that mattered most to her and her students. We talked about how she could spend more of her time investing in what was important and how doing so could reignite her passion for teaching.

When we finished, Karen was visibly relieved. She walked out of our session with a plan for how she would find the time and space in her day to invest in what was important.

If you want to get better at your teaching but feel that district mandates, parental demands, curricular scope, or workplace constraints are getting in the way of your effectiveness, the answer is not to add yet another strategy, process, or responsibility to your plate. Make a "stop doing" list and find ways to eliminate, automate, or delegate what is not as important so that you can focus on what is.

SEPARATE WORK FROM THE REST OF YOUR LIFE

Nuggets of wisdom can come from very unconventional places. My first year of teaching, I worked hard just to keep my head above water. I was teaching three different preps, learning the curriculum, and trying to keep up with the grading. Each day, I would work throughout the day—even through lunch—and then take home a bag full of papers and planning materials. When I got home, I would change into something more comfortable, curl up on the couch, and put in two to three more hours of grading and planning, then fall exhausted into bed by 9:00 pm. The weekends were no better. I spent at least half the weekend (including, I am embarrassed to say, several Saturday nights) trying to catch up.

Not only did I start to resent having to do that much work—work that seemed never to end—but I also began to resent that my home time wasn't my time any more. There was always another paper to grade, another lesson to plan. I hated bringing those papers home because they were a constant reminder of how behind I was. They were a constant source of guilt. If I did something not school related like try to watch a half-hour of television, I couldn't enjoy it because out of the corner of my eye sat that bag of ungraded papers. If I lingered over dinner or talked to a friend on the phone, if I read for pleasure or went to bed early, that bag of papers would sit there condemning me for being a slacker. I hated that bag.

One day as I was dragging my bag of papers home, Nancy, one of the more, shall I say, "eccentric" teachers in my department, stepped out of her classroom and stopped me.

"What are you doing? She demanded.

"I'm going home," I replied, a little taken aback by her tone.

"But why are you taking those papers home?" she asked.

Here we go, I thought to myself. *Another weird conversation with Nancy.* "I have a lot of grading to do," I explained.

"Listen, Nancy, I would love to stay and chat but I should be going." I tried to walk around her but she was blocking my path to the exit.

"Do grocers take groceries home?" she asked with her hands on her hips.

"Uh, no," I replied, not quite sure where she was going with all of these questions.

"Do garbage men take garbage home?" she demanded.

"No."

"Do mailmen take mail home?"

"No."

"Do doctors take home their patients?"

"No."

"Then why are you taking all that work home?" She finished.

As crazy at that conversation seemed, she did make a bit of sense. But how, I wondered, could I get through everything that I was doing if I didn't take the work home?

"If I don't take this work home, I'll never get through it," I explained.

She looked at me and crossed her arms. "Do it here," she nodded and then walked back into her classroom.

I thought about that conversation the entire ride home. Do my work at work? I was already working through my planning periods and lunch. How could I possibly do more? But the next day, I decided to stay late and try to do my grading and planning at school. I worked for an hour after the students were dismissed and deliberately didn't take any papers home that night.

What a difference it made! I went home and actually enjoyed my home for a change. There was no bag of papers mocking me and making me feel guilty. It was wonderful! The next day, no catastrophe happened. Nothing fell apart. In fact, I was in the best mood I had been in for a long time.

That afternoon and for many afternoons after that, I stayed at work late and finished my work there. Because I was working at work, without the distractions and allure of all the things in my home, I found that I was much more efficient and focused. Some nights, I'd spend an hour. Other nights, I might stay for two to three hours, but the moment I drove away from that school building, I was done! I could put work behind me and focus on the rest of my life.

Now I know that staying late won't work for everyone. Some of you have families or classes or other responsibilities that require you leaving work as soon as you're done. But the principle remains. Separate your work life from the rest of your life. Make a clear line of demarcation. Allocate certain times at home when you will work, and set aside a space in your home that is just for work. Close the door literally or metaphorically and do your work. Then, when you are finished, leave your work behind.

Other teachers I know even include a little ritual they do when they are starting work at home and when they finish. Some say a prayer at the beginning and end of their work. Others put their teacher bags in the car when they are finished working, literally putting their work away. One teacher I know who has small children makes a declaration to her family when she is finished working for the day. They applaud and then go enjoy family time. The idea is to draw a clear line between your work and your life. It's one of the best ways I know for keeping your work from *becoming* your life.

CULTIVATE AND NURTURE INTERESTS OUTSIDE OF SCHOOL

You've heard the expression "all work and no play makes Jack a dull boy"? Well, it's true. If all you do is work, you make yourself very, very dull. And having a dull teacher is definitely not good for your students.

I see it all the time—teachers who dedicate their entire lives to teaching. If they aren't in the classroom teaching, they are grading, reading teacher books, going to trainings, planning and replanning lessons, grading papers, designing activities, and so on. Teaching has become their lives. It happens a lot with new

> *It is important to have a life outside of school, not just because it will keep you sane, but because it will make you a better teacher.*

teachers, and I get that. You're so excited about starting your new job or so overwhelmed by all that your new job requires that teaching literally consumes you.

But it is important to have a life outside of school, not just because it will keep you sane, but because it will make you a better teacher. Some of the best lessons I've learned about how to be a good teacher didn't happen at a workshop or during those late nights of grading. Some of the best lessons I learned happened while I was doing something else.

For instance, I remember early in my career I was stuck trying to figure out how to teach my students to think more like writers. I had read several books on the topic, and while those books helped, I still felt that something was missing and I had more to learn. One day, I picked up a book for pleasure and took an afternoon off to read just for me. As I was reading the novel and marveling at the writer's craft, the solution I was looking for hit me. Another time when I was stuck in my teaching, I found the solution while attending the opera. It continues to happen to me. Often when I get stuck in my teaching, my interests outside of teaching offer me a different perspective that helps me get unstuck.

But there's another reason outside interests make you a better teacher. Having a life outside of school makes you a more interesting person, and the more interesting you are as a person, the better a teacher you will be. Students tell me all the time that their favorite teachers are the ones who are passionate not just about their subjects, but about their lives. They love teachers who seem to be whole people much more than the ones whose lives seem to be only about teaching. So go live your life.

WATCH YOUR MONEY

When I first started teaching, I was B-R-O-K-E. Most of my friends had pursued more lucrative careers and were getting new cars, new apartments or houses, and taking great vacations. I was living at home with my parents, barely able to pay off my car loan. A year later, I moved out and almost drowned. I didn't go into teaching for the money, but good grief, I needed at least enough money to live.

Meanwhile, some of the older teachers with whom I worked were encouraging me to start a retirement fund right away. I listened politely, but how on earth could I start putting money away when I had barely enough to live on?

Luckily for me, I had a friend who was an accountant. I called her up one day and told her that I needed her help because I wasn't able to make ends meet. She invited me over and took a long look at my expenses and my pay stub. After a few minutes, I anxiously asked her, "What do you think?" She looked up at me and said, "You need to make more money."

I must have looked distressed because she took one look at my face and immediately tried to reassure me. "Don't worry," she soothed. "I'll help you find a way to make this work." Over the next two hours, she worked and reworked a budget for me. Then she took a pad of paper and at the top of each page wrote my pay date, a list of checks for me to write, an amount I could withdraw in cash, and an amount I had to put away in savings. She even managed to eke out a few dollars so that I could start saving for retirement. I stuck to her budget for the entire school year. It was tough, and at times I was tempted to splurge, but I was glad I stuck with it. It allowed me to have a life.

A big part of having a life is being free from the stress of making ends meet and being able to afford to do the things you want to do. Most books on teacher advice will skip over this part and focus on the intangibles, but the reality is that money is a huge factor in why so many new teachers are stressed out. So, we might as well talk about it. Now, I warn you, this isn't a book on finance; there are already many good ones out there. But I will share with you some really good advice I have gotten over the years from a few wise teachers who have managed to retire millionaires—yes, teachers who retired millionaires!

1. BUILD—AND STICK TO—A BUDGET

First, I learned that it is important to live by a budget, just as my accountant friend helped me to do. I am sure you've heard this many times, but it's worth repeating. Having a budget kept me on track and allowed me to build a nice nest egg in the process. My budget wasn't so taciturn that I wasn't allowed any fun, but being disciplined helped me save up for a house, pay off my car loan early, and get completely debt-free. The peace that came with that freed me up to focus on the things that really mattered to me.

2. CASH IS KING   I learned from an older teacher with whom I worked that cash is king. He paid cash for most things rather than running up his credit card bill, and as a result, he retired very wealthy. He showed me the importance of avoiding debt so that I could use the money I had to buy assets that would appreciate over time. I didn't always follow this advice, but when I didn't, I always regretted it. Even now, I save up for what I want, pay cash when I can, and avoid as much debt as possible. Doing so has allowed me to build a very nice life over time.

3. SAVE!   Save early and often. You'll be amazed at how quickly your savings will build. If you wait until you have more money to save for retirement, it'll be too late. One teacher with whom I worked was a multi-millionaire even though she and her husband were both teachers their entire careers. How did they do it? They paid themselves first. No matter how much they made, they always put away 10 percent of their salaries. Over time, they made good investments and managed their money well, all the while doing work they loved to do. They took great vacations, bought a nice home, drove decent cars, and diligently saved. When they retired, they had over $5 million in cash, investments, and assets. Another teacher couple I know did the same thing, and they have put over

> *If you wait until you have more money to save for retirement, it'll be too late.*

twenty needy students through college over the years. It pays to save.

4. GET A SUMMER JOB IF YOU CAN STAND IT

Work a side gig in the summer if you can. There are a lot of ways to make extra money as a teacher. You can tutor children or adults, write curriculum, lead an extracurricular activity, teach a college course, or any number of other opportunities. I have done them all. Or you can do something entirely different. One teacher I know spends his summers painting cars in an auto body shop because that's his hobby. Another is a yoga instructor on the side because she loves yoga. Whatever it is, working a side gig is a great way to add a little extra money. You can save that money, as many teachers I know do, or you can set aside the money you make from your side job to do something special. I recently met a teacher who is working as a bartender every weekend during the school year so that he can spend six weeks this summer hiking in France.

5. PLAN FOR SUMMERTIME FINANCES

Finally, plan for the summer. I was so focused on trying to make it through my first year of teaching that I didn't make a plan for the summer. I looked up in June and realized the school year was over—and since I hadn't spread my checks out over twelve months, so were my paychecks. I hustled and eked my way through that summer, but what they don't tell you is that it isn't just the summer you have to survive. Many districts operate on a two-week delay, which means that sometimes you are back to school for almost a month before you receive a full paycheck. If you think getting through the summer without pay is bad, try making it through September as well!

After that first year, I started planning for my summer. I set aside money from each paycheck for my summer and September fund. I also started looking for a summer job early on so that I had one by the time summer rolled around. And I planned my vacation early so that I could save for that as well. What a difference a little planning can make! Summer may seem a long way off at the beginning of the year, but it comes around quickly. Plan for it.

~~~

I know that it feels overwhelming right now. You are consumed with teaching. You cannot turn it off in your head. Ever. You spend every waking moment thinking about your classroom. Not only that, there is so much to do. Each day feels like you are constructing everything from scratch. You want to do a good job, but it can seem overwhelming.

I promise you, you can have a life outside of school. Not next year, not in two years when you've got teaching down pat. Right now. You can have a life. And it's important to both you and your students that you carve out some time for yourself to do just that.

CHAPTER 3

YOU CAN SMILE BEFORE CHRISTMAS
WHAT TO DO WITH BAD ADVICE

When you first start teaching, everyone is full of advice:

"Don't smile before Christmas so that the kids know that you're tough and won't try to take advantage of you."
"Be strict at first. You can lighten up later in the year.
"You've got to let them know that you mean it."
"All you have to do is…"

Here's the problem with all that advice when you first start teaching. Most advice seems perfectly logical when you're brand new and trying to figure things out. You won't know that it is bad advice until you've had more experience. So before I share with you some of the worst advice I've heard, I need to show you how to recognize bad advice when you see it.

1. **Bad advice will always make you feel worse, not better**. If you need advice, it's because you are struggling. And if that advice doesn't give you hope, doesn't make you feel better, then it isn't really helpful. Sometimes you'll have to hear tough feedback from others. You will make mistakes and need correction from time to time. We all do. But if that feedback or advice leaves you feeling hopeless, then it isn't really helpful. Even negative feedback should be constructive. If it isn't, it's just bad advice.

2. **Bad advice will be more about the advice giver than about you**. Sometimes people are eager to dispense advice not because they want to help you, but because they want to brag about what they are doing. Good advice is always about you, even when the advice giver uses examples from their own classrooms to help you see a point. Bad advice is never about you.

3. **Bad advice will be something that you cannot use right away**. Sometimes even good, sound advice can be bad advice if you cannot use it right away. If the advice won't work for your teaching style, or is something you can only implement later when you have more experience, or requires you to make a drastic change that you can't make at the moment, it's bad advice.

4. **Bad advice will leave you wondering how to implement it effectively**. Many well-meaning teachers will

give you advice about what you need to do in your classroom. They will say things like, "You need to let your students know that you are in charge." That may be true, but *how* do I do that? Or "You need to establish clear routines." Okay, but what routines? If people give you advice but don't help you figure out how to implement it in *your* classroom with *your* students, it's bad advice.

SOME COMMON PIECES OF BAD ADVICE

Here's some of the worst advice out there and what you can do with it.

BAD ADVICE #1: YOU NEED A TEACHING MAKE-OVER
Whenever you struggle in one area of your teaching, it is tempting to attempt a radical overhaul. In fact, your mentor or whatever teacher advice book you've turned to in desperation may have even suggested an "extreme make-over" as the solution to your problem. Even if it's true and you could use a make-over, it's not likely that it will happen overnight or that you require as huge a change as you think.

Now, I happen to love a good make-over story. I really get into the fairy-tale of it all—that somehow, no matter how profound the problem, all we need is a fairy godmother who will come in and, with a wave of her magic wand, make everything all better.

The truth isn't nearly that exciting. The truth is that it's not the big shifts that will radically change your teaching; it's the small tweaks that do it. Whenever I try to do a teaching make-over of my own practice—or someone else's practice, for that matter—I am always left with a mess. Trying to change everything at once doesn't usually solve the problem you're trying to fix; it just creates a whole bunch of new ones.

I've learned over the years that the best way to solve any teaching problem is to take time to understand the root cause first. Then focus your efforts on fixing the root problem rather than trying to fix everything.

For example, once I really struggled with my seventh-period class. They were seniors, and they had already checked out. I couldn't get them to pay attention, turn in their homework, do work in class, come to class, you name it. They wouldn't listen to me. I tried everything—read a few teacher books, talked to my colleagues, reviewed my notes from my classes—and nothing seemed to work. Finally, someone suggested that I change my entire approach. I was so desperate I thought, *why not?* I worked on my "new attitude" all weekend, and Monday morning, there was a new sheriff in town.

At seventh period, I met my students at the door. I announced that we were going to be doing things differently from now on and explained my new rules and procedures. Then I let them into the classroom. They entered noisily, so I made them get up and go back into the hall and practice again. They got up and went into the hall. *This is gonna work!* I thought excitedly. In the hall, I explained the new rules again and led them into the classroom. Again, they were noisy and rambunctious, so I made them get up and go into the hall again.

You know what happened next, don't you? That's right, the students made it into a game. Going in and out of the classroom was way more interesting to them than untangling the symbolism of Lady Macbeth's hand washing, so they continued to disrupt my brand new routine because they knew that I'd make them do it again. After the fourth or fifth trip in and out of the classroom, I gave up.

They did the same thing to the rest of my "new rules," until my entire new program was vanquished. I was completely demoralized.

When I talked to my mentor about it, he started to chuckle. "Don't laugh at me!" I protested. "I'm humiliated and I don't know what to do."

He rested his hand on my shoulder and said, "That nonsense wasn't ever going to work, and it's good that you learned your lesson in only one day instead of spending weeks investing in your 'new program'" [he used quotes]. "It was too much, Robyn. Like going after a flea with a sledgehammer."

"Un-uh," I shook my head. "This is a big problem and I had to do something big to fix it. Maybe this didn't work, but I need something major. I can't keep going through this."

"Who said that you need something major?" he challenged.

"Come on," I looked incredulously. "That class is a disaster."

"Why?"

I ticked off the challenges. "They don't listen, they don't do their work, they don't respect me, they don't do their homework. I could go on."

"But why are they not doing their work or listening in class?" he asked.

"I don't know," I snapped, frustrated by his line of questioning. "Are you going to tell me that it's my fault?"

"No," he shook his head. "But before you go trying all these new, radical solutions, shouldn't you understand the problem you're trying to fix?"

That sobered me a little. "I don't know how to do that," I finally admitted.

So he showed me. Together we talked about all the things about that particular class that frustrated me. We looked at everything from every angle. He asked me to think about under what conditions my students were most uncooperative, and even asked me to think about any 'bright spots' where they actually *did* do their work. Slowly, a pattern emerged. My students were most likely to do their work when they had a lot of structure. If they sensed even a tiny crack in my plans or my resolve, they would mutiny. But the structure that my students

> *The structure that my students responded to best wasn't a disciplinary crackdown—it had more to do with proper planning. They needed to know that the class had a purpose, a clear routine, and clear outcomes.*

responded to best wasn't a disciplinary crack-down—it had more to do with proper planning. They needed to know that the class had a purpose, a clear routine, and clear outcomes, and then they would get to work. My other classes allowed me a little room, but these students needed every second of the period planned out.

Armed with this new understanding, I made a few small tweaks to the way I ran that class. First, the warm-up was up and ready to go every day when students walked in. At exactly five minutes into the class period, I would take down the warm-up activity and collect their papers. Then I made sure that every day followed the same routine, almost down to the second. If I was tempted to deviate, I would immediately quash the idea. My students needed that kind of structure to stay focused.

Notice that I didn't make a huge shift in my practice— it was the same routine that I used for my other classes. I simply tightened it up during seventh period because that's what the students in that class needed.

Rarely is a radical overhaul needed to fix even the most major problems in your practice. In fact, I have supported thousands of teachers as a coach and mentor, and I have never met one teacher who would have benefited from an extreme makeover. Sure, many of them needed to make major shifts in their practice, but whenever they tried to make more than one or two shifts at a time, their entire practice would fall apart. I've learned that you need to make one shift, and get used to that one, before you make another. Over time your practice will radically improve, but it has to happen one small move at a time.

> *You need to make one shift, and get used to that one, before you make another. Over time your practice will radically improve, but it has to happen one small move at a time.*

BAD ADVICE #2: YOU NEED A BAG OF TRICKS
This one has been around for a long time and has survived largely because it has a ring of truth to it. It's true that every teacher needs a collection of tried and true strategies, activities, and lessons. However, as much as I hate to tell you this, at some point your bag of tricks will let you down. If we apply those "tricks" indiscriminately to

our students, we are not only doing them a huge disservice, we are also doing a disservice to ourselves. Here's why:

Relying on "tricks" keeps us from developing a fully evolved approach to teaching. It keeps us focused on pulling the right trick out of the bag versus developing and operating by a set of principles that govern our practice. For instance, if I'm working with a student who is disengaged, I might immediately revert to my "trick" of calling on him to answer a question. For some students that would work, but for others it would backfire. If instead I used the principle "start where your students are," I would have first tried to figure out why the student was disengaged before reaching for a "trick." Allowing principles of effective instruction to govern your practice will ensure that you respond to each student's individual need.

Relying on a bag of tricks also limits you. One of my favorite sayings is "If the only tool you have is a hammer, every problem looks like a nail." That's the main problem with depending on the tricks in your bag. If you only have a few tricks, you tend to treat everything that arises in the classroom with the strategies you have. If you meet a new challenge for which you have no trick, you will try to use the only tricks you do have, whether or not they actually are best for the situation.

I used to work hard at filling my bag of tricks. I went to conferences and stuffed my suitcase with all the handouts from all the sessions I attended. I read teacher books and took pages of notes. I raided the files of every teacher I met, looking for a new activity, strategy, or worksheet. My file drawers were literally stuffed with strategies I wanted to try, worksheets I thought were cool, and assignments I hoped to give to my students one day.

Over the years, I accumulated a fairly impressive bag of tricks. The problem was that I was so busy collecting tricks that I failed to think about how those tricks would fit into my teaching schedule, match my teaching style, or meet the needs of my students. Sometimes I would shove a cool strategy into a lesson whether it made sense or not. Other times I would default to my teaching style and forget about the tricks altogether, only to kick myself later when I found the folder of materials that would have been perfect for a former lesson if only I'd remembered it was there.

There is no magic in the "bag of tricks." No miracle strategy will work in every situation.

There is no magic in the "bag of tricks." No miracle strategy will work in every situation. It isn't so much what you do but how you *think* that will make the biggest difference. Take time to examine why some techniques work and others don't. Pay attention to the principles behind the strategies rather than just the strategies themselves. Instead of focusing on acquiring more or better tricks, focus on acquiring a better understanding of the principles of effective instruction. Understand that the power is never in the strategy; the power is always in the principles that make the strategy work. Then and only then will you know how to make your bag of tricks work for you and your students.

BAD ADVICE #3: YOU JUST NEED TO WORK HARDER

Teaching is a tough job, especially at first. You are probably working as hard as you can. So when someone tells you that the answer to your early teaching challenges is to work harder, it's easy to become discouraged.

We've all heard the advice "work smarter, not harder," and yet it can be really difficult to figure out how to work smarter when you're working so hard. I remember meeting a brand new third-grade teacher who was one of the hardest-working teachers I had ever seen. Kelly came in early and stayed late. She spent her weekends planning for her students. Every time she faced a new teaching challenge or encountered a student she couldn't quite reach, she'd get to work designing new lessons or creating additional supports. She was very effective in the classroom, and her principal and colleagues thought she had great potential, even as they wondered at her seemingly endless energy. The parents loved her, her students adored her, and she seemed to be well on her way toward becoming a master teacher.

I first met Kelly as I was giving a workshop at her elementary school on differentiated instruction. She sat in the front, took pages of notes, and asked really insightful questions. I could tell that she was eager to learn and would take what she learned and immediately apply it in her own classroom.

So it was a surprise to me when I noticed that Kelly was tearing up a little midway through the morning. The more I talked, the more agitated she seemed to get. I called for a break and walked over to her table to check on her.

"Are you okay?" I asked, concerned.

She nodded and quickly wiped her eyes.

"Did I say something that upset you?" I asked, slightly alarmed.

She shook her head and took a deep breath, trying to collect herself.

"Let's step out into the hall," I suggested.

She followed me out. I waited a few moments while she got herself together. Finally, she apologized, "I'm sorry. I don't know what came over me."

"What did I say that upset you?"

She waved her hand. "Nothing, really. I'm fine."

"I must have said something. What was it?" I pressed.

She sighed and tried to smile. "It's just that you said that I don't have to create all those lessons in order to differentiate."

"Why did that upset you? I meant that to be a relief. I wanted to free you of some of the work you might have been doing," I explained.

"Oh no, it's not that I disagree with you. I see your point," she quickly assured me. "It's just that I've been creating three or four assignments for every lesson I teach all year long. In fact, I just spent two weeks planning three different science labs for my students, collecting three different sets of lab materials, writing three different sets of directions, and setting up three different stations in the classroom. I thought I was being a good teacher. And then today, you tell me that I didn't have to create three different labs. Today you tell me that I only have to create *one* lab and differentiate in that one lab. I worked so hard, and I'm upset because I can't get those two weeks back."

Kelly thought that in order to be a good teacher, she simply needed to work harder. So she worked as hard as she could, and her hard work paid off. She was successful with her students. But she was also exhausted. When she found out that there was a better way, an easier way to accomplish what she was hoping to accomplish through hard work, she felt betrayed.

You will work hard as a teacher. That's the nature of the job. However, there is usually a better, easier way to do most of what you will be asked to do as a teacher. The virtue isn't in the hard work itself; the virtue is in working hard at the right things.

BAD ADVICE #4: ALL YOU HAVE TO DO IS...   Any time advice starts out with "All you have to do is...," look out. Typically you're in for a very pat solution that worked (or not) for someone else but may not work for you. That's because this phrase is flip. It immediately oversimplifies your situation and ignores all nuances.

There are no quick fixes in teaching, no magic cures or miracle methods. What may have worked amazingly for someone else may not work for you. Anyone who starts his or her advice with "All you have to do is..." hasn't taken time to understand *your* situation, your own style of teaching, or the unique nuances of your classroom.

I once had a friend who decided to become a teacher after years as a successful writer and filmmaker. She enrolled in a master's degree program and faithfully applied herself to becoming a master teacher. But once she was hired with a classroom of her own, she really struggled. She turned to her coach and to her principal for help, and they made all kinds of suggestions—most of which didn't work. Several of her colleagues also offered advice, but much of it was totally inapplicable to her situation. Once, she told me that one of her colleagues said, "All you have to do is mean it. You gotta mean it."

"Are you kidding me?" she asked incredulously. "I *do* mean it."

That's the problem with advice that starts with "All you gotta do is ..." Usually, that's not all you have to do, because the person giving the advice is offering a surface solution, not one that gets to the root of your issue.

The best advice takes into account who you are, who your students are, and what you are trying specifically to accomplish. It digs until it finds the root of your problem and then involves you in determining the solution. It's not about what worked for me or for someone else; it's about what will work for you.

BAD ADVICE # 5: FAKE IT 'TIL YOU MAKE IT

A lot of teaching advice out there asks you to mask your personality to be successful. They suggest that you must "Fake it 'til you make it," whether that means pretending to like children you really dislike, feigning proficiency in an area where you are struggling, or affecting expertise to your colleagues or supervisors when they come to observe. Here's the problem with faking it: Who you really are will always leak out.

In my early years of teaching, I often tried to fake it. I was nervous, but I feigned confidence. If I didn't know the answer, I'd make one up. I thought I was fooling my students, but I wasn't. They saw right through me.

Sometimes, they even called me on it.

Once, I was leading a discussion with my eleventh graders, and a student asked a question about the book we were reading. I no longer remember the question, but I do remember how I panicked inside. I didn't know the answer.

But instead of admitting that I didn't know the answer, I made one up.

The student who asked the question accepted my answer and dutifully wrote it down in her notes, but another student said, "You don't really know, do you?"

I was mortified. But since I had started down the "faking it" wormhole, I committed to it.

"What?" I asked incredulously.

"You're just making that up," he pushed back.

I tried to deflect the attention away by getting indignant. "Listen, when we discuss literature, we have to bring all that we know to bear on the discussion. You may not agree with everything, but everyone here has a right to an opinion as long as they can support their opinion. Instead of attacking my opinion, why don't you offer us one of your own?"

The student slumped down in his seat and scowled at me for the rest of the period. I had won the battle but lost the war. It was not one of my finer moments as a teacher.

Years later when I think about that incident, I often wonder what would have happened if I had simply admitted that I didn't know. How much richer would that conversation had been, and what would I have been able to teach that student—all my students really—had I not faked it and just admitted that I didn't know the answer?

I understand why people suggest that you fake it until you make it. When you're nervous, intimidated, or unsure, it feels bet-

> *Vulnerability makes you real to your students. It keeps you in a place of humility and authenticity.*

ter to fake confidence, or surety, than to admit that you don't have the answer and risk looking vulnerable in front of your students. If your students sense any weakness, you figure, they'll take advantage and eat you alive. But vulnerability isn't the same as weakness. Vulnerability, when done right, can actually be a very strong position to take with your students.

Vulnerability makes you real to your students. It keeps you in a place of humility and authenticity. You show your students that you don't have to know everything and invite them to discover the answer together with you. You also model to them how to be vulnerable themselves and still take risks in the classroom.

Authority built on knowing everything and never being wrong is shaky. It can easily collapse. It is staked on fear and attempts to hide your weaknesses rather than turning your weaknesses into strengths. It isn't real.

Authority built on vulnerability, on taking risks, on trying and failing and trying again, on being your authentic self, is real. It lasts. It garners hard-won respect.

It's uncomfortable, but if you want a classroom where real learning takes place, it's necessary.

Faking it makes you hide from discomfort. Vulnerability forces you to lean into discomfort and ultimately master it. Faking it is about hiding from the risk that is teaching. Being vulnerable is about taking the risk. And when your students see you fighting and learning and getting better at teaching each day, they learn something important. They learn that it is okay to take risks themselves. They learn that your classroom is a safe place to learn, to make mistakes, and to try again. They learn that it's okay to be themselves because you've already shown them yourself, your true self.

❧

Throughout this chapter, I have emphasized the importance of finding your own path, of becoming yourself—your very best self—and developing your own teaching style, your own approach to teaching. I've talked at length about why it is important and shared some advice about how to find it. What I haven't told you is how very hard that process will be.

If you're a new teacher, you're probably receiving a lot of support and advice right now. In fact, you may feel like you are receiving too much advice. Everyone seems to know what you need to do to be successful in your classroom.

With all this advice, it becomes even harder to find your own way. Your principal tells you one thing, your coach offers a different solution, your colleagues chime in with a third. Even your friends who aren't teachers make suggestions and your family offers pointers. Everyone has an opinion.

To make matters worse, someone hands you a book on teaching that lays out a plan of action and makes everything look easy. Or you go online searching for help and are overwhelmed by the proliferation of advice out there. It's hard to know what advice to take, to whom you should listen, and what will ultimately work for you.

Here's my advice: At some point, you have to listen to your gut.

As trite as that may sound, it's the one thing that I find new teachers rarely do. You listen to everyone else except yourself. You may not even believe that you know enough to have a "gut" yet. You want to get it right or you feel pressure to do what your supervisors say so that you can get a good evaluation and keep your job. Maybe you have tried to go with your gut and failed.

But these first few years of teaching are important not only because you are learning how to become a teacher. You're also learning how to develop your *teacher sense*— that sixth sense all great teachers have that shows them exactly what to do in the moment to best help their students learn. If you drown out your own gut in favor of everyone else's advice, you'll never develop a teacher sense of your own.

At the end of the day, it's *your* classroom. Yes, you have standards to meet, observations and evaluations to survive, test scores to achieve, and an intense amount of scrutiny from your students and their families. I'm not suggesting that you go rogue and do your own thing in spite of the expectations of your supervisors and your district. I'm also not suggesting that you ignore the advice that's out there. Some of it will be pretty good and will save you trouble in the long run. I am simply suggesting that you sift every bit of advice through your own emerging understanding of your students, and your own developing teaching style, and then do what is best for students. A friend of mine always says in his workshops that participants should adapt—not adopt—his advice. He's right. The best thing to do with advice, good or bad, is to test it with your gut and adapt it to make it work for you.

CHAPTER 4

YOU CAN DESIGN GREAT LESSONS
HOW TO TACKLE PLANNING

My first year of teaching actually started in January. I had chosen to go straight through school to earn my master's degree before I started teaching, and I finished my program in December. I interviewed at a few places, and I was offered a job teaching eleventh- and twelfth-grade English. The department chair had decided to retire in the middle of the school year but hadn't told his students or any but his closest colleagues and his principal. He left on a Friday and I started that Monday.

My first day on the job happened to be in the middle of semester exams. All of the teachers in my department were administering or grading exams, which left me time to get used to my classroom and to try to digest my curriculum. I had three preps—honors English 11, on-level English 11, and English 12. At the time, there wasn't much of a curriculum available, but the departing department chair gave me three binders with ancient mimeographed curriculum documents as well as a few textbooks and wished me luck.

I had no idea what I was doing, and there was no one in the department to talk to. Although I had learned how to write lesson plans in my undergraduate education program and had submitted a unit plan or two in my graduate program, I realized at that moment that I really had no idea how to begin. I made myself busy copying handouts for my first day and cobbling together a few lessons to get myself started.

I got through my first day relieved that the kids didn't seem to notice that I had no idea what I was doing. Someone gave me a lesson-planning book, so I quickly abandoned my carefully typed, three-page lesson plans and each night scribbled my agenda for the next day in my plan book. I managed to stay a few pages ahead of the kids in the textbook, but much of my teaching was hit or miss. Sometimes I delivered a great lesson, but it certainly didn't happen consistently. I'd write lesson objectives after I wrote the lesson, or I'd plan a lesson and then locate standards that seemed to fit it afterward. Sometimes I planned an entire unit around a favorite book or a cool activity I'd read about, and afterward went back and tried to make it fit with my curriculum or standards. There were even times when I just followed the curriculum guide without really understanding why it was arranged that way or how it was moving my students toward the standards. Mostly, I was just trying to keep my head above water.

To be honest, I taught that way for the first couple of years of my career. And I can tell you from experience that it's an exhausting way to teach. It wasn't until I attended a summer workshop on lesson planning that I really learned how to design great units, and I do not exaggerate when I say that it was a life-altering experience. Simply thinking through my entire unit in advance and focusing every lesson toward a unit goal gave my teaching focus. Not only that, it immediately made my lessons more coherent and my students' performance significantly better on the common assessments.

Right now, you're probably trying to figure out the standards, benchmark assessments, core curricula, and so on. You may be drowning under a weight of curriculum documents or completely baffled by curriculum maps. Perhaps you're trying to distinguish the difference between a power standard and sub-standards while also trying to design assessments and lessons that are directly tied to the standards. Perhaps you've been handed a curriculum that you must follow exactly, with no wiggle room for designing your own lessons. Maybe you face periodic benchmark assessments and worry whether your lessons are adequately preparing students for these assessments. Or maybe you're spending hours each night preparing elaborate lesson plans that conform to your district's preferred planning template. Lesson and unit planning are fraught with all kinds of challenges. But no matter what particular challenge you're facing, you *can* plan amazing units and lessons. Here's how.

ASK WHY FIRST

One of the hardest questions I ever ask a teacher is "Why are you teaching this?" In most cases, the honest answer is "I don't really know." But if you don't understand why you're teaching what you are teaching, you can't teach it well.

At the beginning of your career, it's hard to understand the "why" of what you're teaching. You're too busy trying to figure out the "what"—what content, what materials, what assessments, what accommodations, and so on. But taking time to understand, at least on a global level, why you are teaching what you're teaching is the first step to figuring out the *what* and the *how* of teaching.

As I mentioned, I started teaching in the middle of a school year. I had just three days to digest the curriculum before starting. Three days to plan for three preps on two grade levels. Since I had no idea where to begin, I just picked what I thought was a good place (something similar to the lessons I had taught during my student teaching) and started there. For me, those first few weeks were about staying ahead of my students and making sure they had something to do each day. I assumed I would figure out the curriculum later.

I wish I had started with the *why* first. It would have made my first year so much easier. Unfortunately, it wasn't until my third year of teaching that I learned to "start with the why." Our district had dramatically changed our curriculum, so I had to scrap most of the lessons I'd created over the past year and a half and create all new ones.

That summer, I attended a two-hour workshop—the one, as I said before, that changed my life. The presenter talked about planning with the end in mind. He talked about the importance of knowing what the essential understanding of each unit was before you taught it. I was captivated and inspired. I went home that night and pulled out my new curricula and immediately started trying to tease out the essential understandings. I asked myself, "Why am I teaching this?" "Why is this important?"

> *I realized that when I answered the* why *first, the* what *and* how *took care of themselves.*

What I discovered was, quite frankly, amazing. First, I realized that when I answered the *why* first, the *what* and *how* took care of themselves. Once I understood why I was teaching poetry, for instance, I then understood which poems would work with my unit, what concepts I needed to teach, how I needed to assess my students, and what mastery looked like. My units suddenly became crystal clear.

Second, by asking why first, I was able to better understand my standards and why they were important. That helped me put my standards in kid-friendly language and really explain them to my students. Third, I enjoyed the planning process much more once I understood the why. The curriculum suddenly made sense. And the process of teasing out the why reconnected me to my own passion about my subject and about learning in general. Finally, I found that when I taught my units, I did so with much more passion and focus. I knew what was important and therefore could make the units more relevant to my students.

That fall, I came back to my students with a renewed sense of purpose and passion. Rather than being a chore, teaching was fun! It was exciting to see my students "get it," especially once I understood exactly what they were supposed to be getting. And rather than be saddled by a new curriculum that siphoned off all my creativity and passion for my subject, I was empowered by my curriculum to teach the way that I knew was best for my students and still meet the demands of the standards, the pacing guide, and the benchmark assessments.

This is why when I work with teachers I always start with the why. Why are you teaching area and volume? Why are you teaching the Reconstruction? Why are you teaching root words? The periodic table? Why is learning the parts of speech, or the rules of basketball, or place value, or the difference between an acute and a right angle, so important? I always find that when teachers really think through the why first, planning goes more easily, their teaching is more coherent, and they're much more passionate about what they do. I hope that you will take some time to think about why you are teaching what you are teaching. Trust me. It's totally worth it.

FOCUS ON YOUR STANDARDS

Understanding the standards can seem overwhelming. With everything else that you have to do to create lesson plans, assessments, and other learning materials, it's easy to treat the standards as an afterthought, another hurdle you have to leap over, rather than make them the cornerstone of your planning.

But the standards are critical to ensuring that your students are ready for state assessments and that you're teaching your material at grade level. If you don't start with your standards and make them the cornerstone of your planning process, not only will your lesson plans be all over the place, your students won't be prepared for state assessments or for the next grade level.

Recently, I worked with a new teacher who had come to teaching through an alternative certification program. Sean was smart, knew his subject matter, and was passionate about helping his Special Education students meet standards on the state tests. He diligently wrote lesson plans each day according to his district's format, but he struggled to cover all the material required by the curriculum. When we sat down to work on his plans, Sean showed me his process.

"So basically, I follow the textbook," he said, spreading out his plans. "The problem is that I can't cover everything in here. My students need more time to get stuff, and some of them are so far behind that I have to teach them things that are not in the book just so that they can get the stuff that *is* in the book."

"Where are your standards?" I asked.

Sean flipped open his laptop and navigated to the state's website. "Usually, I plan my lessons first," he explained. "Then, once I'm done, I check the state website and pick which standards apply."

I nodded. Many teachers I'd worked with used the same process. "Is the state test based on the textbook or the standards?" I asked.

"The standards, I think," he answered tentatively.

"Then shouldn't you start with the standards rather than the textbook?" I prodded.

"But if I did that, I'd be all over the place. These standards don't seem to have any order to them."

I agreed—the standards *were* all over the place. "Well," I picked up a blank piece of paper and drew a table. "Let's get the standards organized so that they make sense."

We spent the next hour going through the standards and organizing them in a logical order. We often referred to the textbook to help us figure out a logical sequence. When we were finished, we had created a chart that ordered his standards and connected each standard to the appropriate chapters in the textbook.

"Now," I said as I sat back and surveyed our work, "Each of these standards will become a unit."

Sean looked at me quizzically. "I don't understand."

I pointed at the first standard on the chart. "This standard here will become the basis of your unit one. The next standard will be your unit two, and so on. You'll create a unit plan for each standard and a unit assessment that will assess each standard. That way, you can make sure that your students have mastered each standard and are ready for the state assessment in the spring."

From there, I helped him plan his unit. We took into account the extra time and material he would have to cover to backfill his students' missing background knowledge and skills. Then we mapped all of his units onto a calendar and made adjustments to be sure that he could cover the most important material by the time the state test was administered. When we were finished, he leaned back in his chair and sighed.

"That was a lot of work," I smiled sympathetically.

"Yeah," he agreed. "But for the first time I feel like I actually know what I'm doing."

That's the power of working from your standards rather than from your curriculum guide. If you end planning with your standards, you have no real way of knowing whether you'll meet all of them. But if you start with the standards and organize your curriculum around them, you can be sure that you're teaching the most important material and teaching on grade level.

PLAN AHEAD

I know it's hard to plan ahead when you're new to the curriculum and new to teaching, but it's important if you want to keep your sanity. By "ahead," I don't mean that you need to have lesson plans for every subject you teach by day one. But you should map out at least your first grading period so that you have a sense of where you're going.

It's a bit of an up-front investment to map everything out ahead of time, but it will save you a lot of frustration later on. If you have a map—an overview of where you're headed—you can write daily lesson plans more quickly, make adjustments in your plan without sacrificing the most important parts of your curriculum, and better align your materials and assessments to the standards.

Early in my career, I discovered the power of mapping out my units ahead of time. The first time I did this, I had been given a new curriculum. I spent the latter part of the summer mapping it out and really unpacking my standards. I used that map the entire year to help me stay on track, make sure that I covered everything I was responsible for covering, and help me stay focused. Although I had to make adjustments to the map, making those adjustments was a lot easier than having to go back to square one every time I started a new unit during the school year.

Sometimes you don't have the entire summer to digest your curriculum and map out your year. Sometimes you're forced to build the plane as you are flying it. That was the case with Marjorie, a brand new teacher who approached me after a training I had given. Marjorie had come to teaching later in life, after a fruitful career as a real estate agent. She was bright, committed, and totally overwhelmed.

She waited quietly after the workshop to speak to me. Once everyone else was gone, she asked for a few minutes of my time. She had such a sense of urgency about her that I invited her to sit down.

As soon as she was seated, she began to cry. "I'm sorry," she apologized, as she fished in her purse for a tissue.

"It's okay," I assured her. "What's going on?"

"I'm just so totally overwhelmed," she began. "I am a new teacher and I work hard. But no matter how hard I work, I can't seem to keep up. I teach third grade, and I have to teach them everything, and I can barely stay a few pages ahead of them. I'm drowning," she sobbed.

I'd seen it before. Many times new teachers begin to become overwhelmed near the end of the first grading period. A friend of mine calls it the "October breakdown."

I asked her a few more questions and then suggested, "Marjorie, the reason you are so overwhelmed is that you don't have a plan. You're trying to plan lessons with no real understanding of how they hang together or where you're heading. You're just trying to keep your head above water."

"But what else can I do?" she protested. "I'm working as hard as I can just to stay two steps ahead of my kids. I can't do any more."

"I'm sure you are working hard," I assured her. "I am suggesting that you work *differently*."

"Differently?" she looked up from her tissue. "How?"

"You need to map everything out."

"But I have curriculum maps," she protested. "They give them to us and then check to see that we are on the right page of the map on the right day. Those maps are part of why I'm so stressed out. I feel like I can't stop and help my students understand everything. I just have to keep rolling along," she swept her hand dramatically. "I hate those maps."

"Have you taken the time to study those maps, understand how they work, make them make sense to you? Or are you just following them?"

"I'm just trying to keep up."

"Well, that's the problem. You need to make those maps make sense for you *and* for your students."

"I wish I could," she sighed. "But I don't have the luxury of time for that."

"Do you have any leave?" I asked.

"Leave?"

"Yes, leave. Can't you take a day off so that you can buy yourself some time?"

"I guess. Can I really do that? Can I really take a day off work?"

I laughed. "Marjorie, you're drowning. You're not taking a day off so that you can sit around and eat bonbons. You need time to collect yourself and figure things out. It's your leave—you're allowed to use it."

She looked at me and weighed what I was saying. I continued, "If you took a day off, you could spend that day really unpacking all those curriculum documents and making them make sense. Then you could create a road map for yourself that would get you at least to the end of the semester. Your map would of course align with the curriculum maps you've been given, but it would be simpler, easier to understand. You could even map it out on your calendar so that you'd know what you are doing each day. However it makes sense to you. Then, when you sat down to write lesson plans each night or week or whatever, you wouldn't have to spend all that time trying to figure out what to do; your map would show you. You could just sit down and write your plans."

Marjorie considered my suggestion, but I could tell she was still struggling with the idea of taking a day off.

"You need this," I urged. "You're drowning."

She nodded slowly. "I'll talk to my principal and put in for leave next Monday. That way I can get started over the weekend and perhaps map things out for the year."

"Maybe," I said cautiously. "But don't set yourself up for more frustration. This will take time. Just aim for mapping things out for the first semester. Winter break is coming up, so you can use that time to take care of the second semester," I warned. "Take things a little bit at a time."

And that's exactly what she did. She took that day off and worked on unpacking her curriculum and mapping it out for the semester. It took some time, but she returned to school with a new sense of purpose and a renewed sense of passion.

That's what taking the time to unpack your curriculum and mapping out your process will do for you. It will give you a sense of control. You'll know where you are headed and can make better decisions on the

> *Planning day to day is exhausting. Having a sense of where you are going and planning according to your map is empowering.*

spot. And lesson planning is much easier because you have a context for each lesson. It's an investment, but it is worth it. Planning day to day is exhausting. Having a sense of where you are going and planning according to your map is empowering. Take time to map out your curriculum and make it make sense to you.

DON'T TRY TO COVER EVERYTHING

As a new teacher I thought that if it was in the curriculum, it had to be taught. The problem is that most curriculum documents are so bloated that it's difficult to cover everything or to allot the same amount of time to every assignment. What's more, covering the curriculum does not guarantee that the students will meet all of the standards. Once I realized this, I began to focus on the standards and on helping my students reach the standards rather than just cover the curriculum. Doing so gave me more time to teach what really mattered and more flexibility to adjust my teaching based on my students' needs.

Still, it's hard not to feel the pressure to cover everything. I see teachers struggling with this all the time. I remember working with one teacher who didn't want my help. I was there to help Peter make his lessons more rigorous, but when I walked into his classroom, I could tell that I wasn't welcome.

"So, what can I help you with today?" I asked as I took a seat across from Peter at a table in the back of the classroom.

"If you really want to 'help' me," he began sarcastically, "tell me how I'm gonna cover all of this by the end of May." He dropped the curriculum documents he was holding onto the table dramatically.

I eyed the thick document and asked, "How long does it usually take you to cover this material?"

Peter smirked and leaned back in his chair, crossing his arms over his chest. "Eight weeks."

It was the second week of April. With state testing and other end-of-the-year activities, we had about five weeks. Maybe.

I picked up the curriculum document and skimmed it quickly. It included a ton of vocabulary, several projects, a few tests, and quite a bit of information to cover. I didn't really know the content, so I couldn't rely on my subject-area expertise to help him. Instead, I went back to the principle of quality over quantity and asked a question: "What are your need-to-knows and what are your nice-to-knows?"

"What?"

"Your need-to-knows," I repeated. "What things do your students absolutely have to know?"

Peter looked at me like I was the dumbest person he had ever met. "All of it. They need to know all of it. It's in the curriculum, and it will be on the test."

I could tell he was getting annoyed with me, so I quickly explained, "There is some research that says that most curriculum is bloated. Not everything in your curriculum will be on the state test. In fact, some say that about 80 percent of your curriculum is essential, and about 20 percent of your curriculum is 'nice-to-know.' So if we can figure out your 'need-to-knows' and your 'nice-to-knows,' I think we can figure out how to get all of this done in the time we have left."

He thought for a moment and then said, "But what if you're wrong?"

"But what if I'm right?" I smiled. "Look, you've got to work with me anyway for the rest of the planning period. Why not try this and see if it makes sense?"

Peter reluctantly agreed, and we got to work. We went through his curricular documents and started with the *why*—Why was this unit important, and what were the standards and essential ideas that students absolutely needed to know? From there, we took every activity, every vocabulary word, every item of content, and every skill and divided them into two columns: 80 percent we put in the need-to-know column; 20 percent we put in the nice-to-know column. It took us about thirty minutes to get through everything, but at the end, we had Peter's curriculum divided.

Next, I explained that everything in the need-to-know column had to be taught to mastery. But anything in the nice-to-know column could be simply presented to students so that they were familiar with it, but they didn't have to learn it to mastery.

From there, we took out a calendar and quickly mapped out what content, concepts, and skills would be taught on what days, and by the time the period was over, Peter had a general plan.

"I didn't think you could do it," he said, shaking his head as he looked over his plan.

I grinned, "It sounds like you were setting me up to fail."

He looked up and admitted, "I was in a way. I thought there was no way I could cover everything in the time I had left, and I have no problem admitting that I was pretty mad about that. But with these need-to-knows, I realize now that I could have probably

Your students will actually do better if you don't cover everything, or, at least, if you don't cover everything with equal weight.

covered stuff a lot more deeply throughout the year if I hadn't been so worried about covering everything."

It sounds counterintuitive, but your students will actually do better if you don't cover everything, or, at least, if you don't cover everything with equal weight. Take time to determine your need-to-knows and your nice-to-knows, and spend more time on your need-to-knows. Not only will your teaching have more coherence, your students will learn much more deeply and be far better prepared for their assessments later on.

BE PREPARED, BUT DON'T OVER-PREPARE

When I was preparing to become a teacher, many of my professors warned me that I should plan twice as much as I needed, just in case. And to this day, I believe in having a plan B. However, many times we over-prepare as a way of reducing our own anxiety about teaching. We feel more secure knowing that we have our plans, and backup plans, and backups for the backups. But over-preparing to feel more secure is a trap. Not only does over-preparation fool us into thinking that we have everything under control, it often makes us so locked into our lesson plans that we don't leave spaces for our students to occupy and cocreate their learning experience.

Early in my teaching career, I prided myself on my preparation. I carefully mapped out units, created detailed lessons planned down to the minute, and prepared plenty of material to keep my students occupied for the entire class period. It was all very impressive, believe me.

One day, I was delivering one of my carefully prepared lessons in which I was leading a class discussion. I had mapped out my discussion questions ahead of time and estimated how long the discussion should last. About halfway through the discussion, I asked a question that really piqued my students' interest. Hands shot up, and students who were usually quiet eagerly joined the conversation. Students were making all kinds of connections and thinking deeply, and they were really engaged, but I kept worrying that we would never get to the rest of the questions on my list, so after each student's comment, I tried to get the class redirected to the next question.

My students ignored me. They kept going back to the question that really intrigued them. At one point, I said, "Guys, look. We still have a lot of questions to discuss here. We need to move on."

One student sucked his teeth and rolled his eyes, "We finally have a good discussion and you want to cut it short," he complained. The other students chimed in and agreed.

I saw the mutiny unfolding in front of me and acquiesced. The students continued with the discussion, but I couldn't enjoy it or even facilitate it. I was too busy stewing over my derailed plans.

At the end of the day, I complained about my failed lesson to my colleague next door. "Now I'm going to have to push back my plans for tomorrow so that I can get through these questions," I whined.

"Robyn, what was the point of your questions?" he asked gently.

"To get the students to discuss the novel and come to their own insights about what they read. I wanted them to think about what they read and make some connections between the text and their own lives."

He looked at me for a moment and waited for it to sink in. "Did that happen?"

"Yes, but …" It finally dawned on me. I smiled sheepishly. They *had* made connections. They were engaged and excited about what they had read. They were thinking deeply. And I had missed it all because I was so worried about getting through my lesson plan. I can't say that was the last time I made that mistake. I still catch myself sometimes focusing on my plans rather than on the people in front of me. It's a delicate balance—you do need to keep the class moving toward your goal, but you have to be open to the possibility that getting to the goal may take a different path than the one that you have so carefully scripted.

On paper, learning is a neat and linear process in which students proceed from

> *You mustn't script every moment in the classroom so tightly that you leave no room for that spontaneous teachable moment, no space for students to actively cocreate their learning experience.*

point A to point B in an orderly and timely fashion. In reality, learning is much messier than that. No matter how well you plan, your students will derail those plans from time to time. That doesn't mean that you never plan; it just means that you must understand that your plans are just that—plans.

To manage this balance and avoid the trap of over-preparation, focus on your goal, not the steps you've planned to meet your goal. It's important to plan carefully, but you mustn't script every moment in the classroom so tightly that you leave no room for that spontaneous teach-able moment, no space for students to actively cocreate their learning experience. Prepare, yes. But leave enough flexibility in your plans so that you can be fully present in your classroom and open to opportunities for learning that may not have been factored into your plans.

STICK TO THE PLAN, NOT THE SCRIPT

I was observing a fourth-grade classroom recently where the teacher stood in front of the students and basically read the lesson from the teacher's guide. The students gamely followed along, trying to answer the questions he read and perform the tasks he recited. They were clearly eager to learn. But in spite of sticking to the script, the lesson fell flat, and students were confused about what they were supposed to be learning.

When I met with the teacher later that day to provide feedback, I asked him why he taught that lesson. He said, "Because it's in the teacher's guide."

I nodded. "I see that. But why did you choose to use the lesson in the teacher's guide?"

He shrugged. "I don't have a choice."

"Of course you do," I insisted.

"No I don't," he shook his head. "I have to use the same plans as everyone else."

"You have to teach the same standards and have the same objectives as everyone else," I clarified. "Your district policy doesn't say anything about teaching the same exact lesson as everyone else."

He stared at me for a second. "I thought I had to teach the lesson this way."

"Did the lesson work?" I asked.

He shook his head. "Not really," he sighed. "But I thought I didn't have a choice."

"How would you have taught that lesson if you could have done whatever you wanted?" I asked.

"If I could have done what I wanted?"

"Yes," I nodded as I closed the teacher's guide. "How did you want to teach that lesson?"

He thought for a moment. "Well, for starters, I wouldn't have done the warm-up. It was silly, and my kids already knew that information."

"What would you have done instead?"

"I would have had them start right away with the story, get them plunged into it. Then, I would have divided them into groups to figure out for themselves how dialogue was punctuated. Notice the patterns and keep a record of what patterns they saw."

"Go on," I prompted.

He was starting to get more animated. "And then I would have made a running list and had them write some dialogue as a class using the rules on the list. When we ran into problems of interpretation, we would add to the list of rules. By the time we were finished, we would have had a really good understanding of dialogue—both how to punctuate it and how to write it."

He went on to explain the rest of the lesson he would teach and how it would do a better job of getting students to the standards. The more he talked, the more excited he became. When he finished, I simply asked, "Why not teach *that* lesson?"

He looked me directly in the eye. "I'd love to. I just didn't know that I was allowed."

You are allowed. Even if you're handed a tightly scripted set of lesson plans with the expectation that you teach lessons the exact same way on the same day as every other teacher in your grade, it is still important to take time to unpack those lessons and tweak them so that you understand what you are teaching and why you are teaching it. Once you understand the connection between the activities and the standards, you can choose to teach the lesson as is, or tweak it to better help your students reach the standards. Either way, you're the teacher and you must decide how to best help your students reach the standards. You must adjust the lesson to better meet your students' needs.

What's *not* okay is teaching the lesson as is, without thinking it through first. What is not okay is depending on the script and not taking time to unpack the standards for yourself. No matter how well-written a lesson plan is or how carefully scripted it is, it won't work unless you understand it. So take time to understand your lessons for yourself. That way, even if you choose to follow the script, you'll also be following the plan.

Lesson and unit planning is perhaps one of the most important things you do as a teacher. In fact, much of our work happens during the planning process. And yet, planning can be so overwhelming, so time-consuming, and so confusing, that we end up skipping over the most important parts.

I would argue that planning is more about *you* than it is about the students. The better you understand what you are going to teach

> *Planning is more about you than it is about the students. The better you understand what you are going to teach that day, the better you will be able to teach your students.*

that day, the better you will be able to teach your students. If you skimp on planning, you cheat yourself as much as you cheat your students.

Planning done right gives you confidence. You know exactly what you're teaching and why you are teaching it. Planning right helps your students trust you because they can sense that you know where you're going and have thought through how to help them get there with you.

CHAPTER 5

YOU CAN FIND COMMON GROUND
WORKING WITH PARENTS

One of the most intimidating things about teaching is working with parents. Although we all dream of easy, cooperative, positive relationships with parents, unfortunately, that isn't always possible right away. Sometimes you'll have to work at it. Here are a few ways to make your relationships with parents and guardians much more productive.

BE PROACTIVE

By the time a parent contacts you they're usually already frustrated. And angry. And annoyed. At that point, you will spend most of your time trying to defuse their frustration rather than resolve the original issue, which may be buried under a pile of other issues that have accumulated throughout the year. Thus, if you really want to ensure a positive interaction with parents, it's best if you initiate it.

When I first started teaching, I avoided dealing with parents. When parents contacted me, I'd cringe. Usually, they were not calling with good news. By seeing them as adversaries, or at least a nuisance I wanted to avoid, I created more problems with parents than I solved. Once I learned to see parents as my partners, to keep them informed about what was going on in my class, and to bring them into the loop early in the process, I found that parents were my best allies. As a result, even when we disagreed on a course of action, we were more likely to work out a plan that we both could support. Here are some ways to proactively develop your partnership with parents:

1. **The all-important introductory letter.** The first way to be proactive is to make good use of your introductory letter or Back-to-School Night presentation. I gave my students' parents a realistic sense of how things would go in my classroom over the year, including the amount of homework they could expect, the types of assignments I would give, and the classroom policies I would enforce. That way, parents knew clearly the kind of teacher I was and what they could expect from me throughout the year. Managing expectations early is key to ensuring that parents feel comfortable and trust you with their children.

2. **Don't wait.** Initiate contact with parents at the first sign of trouble rather than waiting until students have been failing for some time. Have a plan to nip trouble in the bud early so that you can get students quickly back on track.

3. **Reach out with good news.** Don't only call about the bad stuff. If possible, let your first few communications with parents be about positive aspects of their child's performance so that parents don't begin to dread hearing from you.

4. **Talk to parents before the student does.** Finally, get to the parents before the child does. That way, you and the parent can present a united front with the student. If I have had an interaction with a student, I try to call home as soon as I can so that the first story the parents hear is mine. That way, we can get on the same page and work together. If your student tells the story first, he may twist the story to the point where the parent is uninterested in hearing your side. If you're the first to tell the story, you can present it in a fair and neutral light and give parents time to start thinking about the solutions to the challenge before they speak to their child later that day.

Being proactive doesn't entirely prevent challenges with parents, but it does significantly minimize them. I've seen many problems escalate because the teacher wasn't proactive and have seen a lot of parent interactions work effectively because the teacher was proactive.

EMPOWER PARENTS TO ADVOCATE FOR THEIR STUDENTS THE RIGHT WAY

Parents want to advocate for their children. It's Parenting 101. And yet, most parents don't have any idea how to navigate the school culture and get what's best for their children. They tend to use strategies that they know—things that worked when the department store over-charged them for an item or when they wanted to lower their cable bill. They yell, they threaten, and they get what they want. Although the tactics that work in the consumer space aren't appropriate in a school context, many parents don't know any other way to advocate for what they want or need.

In this situation, it's up to you to educate and empower parents with appropriate strategies they can use to advocate for their students. One of the best ways I know to empower parents is to use what I call a *proactive intervention plan*. Basically, this is a plan that anticipates when and how students might struggle in my class and provides supports up front, before they drop into a freefall of failure. I used Back-to-School Night to share the plan with parents—I'd tell parents what red flags I was looking for and what they should be looking for at home. I told them when they should contact me and what supports I would guarantee that their students received. I also shared several strategies for how they could provide supports at home.

Implementing a proactive intervention plan made all the difference. When parents contacted me, it wasn't stemming from some vague sense of unease about the way things were going for their students in my classroom; they contacted me with specific "red flags" they observed at home. Often, the information they shared was information I didn't know and helped round out the picture I had formulated of the student in the classroom. By giving parents red flags to watch for and a way to communicate with me about them, we could have a very productive conversation about how to best help their students succeed. Parents were always grateful to be given a way to communicate about their students, and I was able to formulate cooperative relationships with parents.

In another school where I worked, we went a step further and hosted several "study skills" nights for parents. During those events, we taught parents the difference between helping their students with homework and doing it for them, strategies for supporting good study habits, how to manage the homework schedule, and ways parents could support more rigorous and independent thinking for their students. We even explained some of the content (especially the new math the students were learning), so that parents could help their students at home. Thus we empowered parents with ways that they could support homework at home, and we saw an increase in the amount of homework that was completed and turned in. I've seen other schools that provide this type of advice for parents on their school web sites or in letters home. I've even seen teachers send instructions home to parents on how they can support their child's homework. The more you show parents how to support their students, the better support you'll get from them.

REMEMBER, THEY'RE NOT *YOUR* PARENTS EVEN IF THEY'RE OLD ENOUGH TO BE

I was twenty-three years old when I started teaching. My students were high school seniors who were only four or five years younger than I. Most of their parents were old enough to be my parents. Some of their parents were *older* than my own parents. I found this a little intimidating.

What made things worse was that I was reared in a very traditional home. I never called my parents' friends by their first names, and I was taught to respect my elders by giving them due deference. So, when I first

> *That focus on my students immediately put me on the same level as their parents.*

became a teacher and had to relate to my students' parents, I faced a dilemma: My rearing insisted that I defer to them as my elders, but my job demanded that I interact with them as peers.

How did I get over it? By focusing on my students rather than on their parents. I focused on what they needed, and I advocated for them. That focus on my students immediately put me on the same level as their parents, since we were both adults tasked with helping this student, and we both wanted the best for the child. Whenever I focused on the parents, the disparity between our ages was glaring. But when I focused on the students and what was best for them, there was little difference between me and their parents. Don't be intimidated by the parents. Remember that you and they are partners working for the best for their children.

KEEP IN MIND THAT THEY WANT WHAT'S BEST FOR THEIR CHILDREN

We tend to treat parents like the enemy. When we prepare for a meeting with a parent, it's like preparing for battle. What we often fail to realize is that we're on the same side.

While you may disagree about how to get there, make no mistake, you're both trying to achieve the same result— what's best for the student. If you remind yourself of this often during parent meetings, not only will it make the meeting less adversarial, it will help you come up with solutions that you may not have considered before.

I had to learn this lesson several times over the years. One instance in particular sticks out:

I had a student who was presenting a significant behavior problem in my classroom. Not only was he disrespectful to me, he was distracting other students by talking to them when they were trying to work. More than once, he derailed a lesson and got the entire class off track. What made him particularly challenging was that he was a really smart kid and would do his own work. He was earning a solid B in my class.

His behavior was getting worse, so I called his mother in for a conference. I wanted her support in getting him to behave in my classroom by reinforcing my rules and expectations at home. I thought I had it all figured out. I had given the matter a great deal of thought, and I had the plan lined up and ready to go. My only problem was to convince my student's mother that this was the best choice for her son.

But the mother had also worked out a plan. She had also given the matter a great deal of consideration and had her own ideas about what needed to be done. We sat in the meeting arguing over our plans and completely lost sight of what was best for the student. We were too busy trying to prove that our plan was the right one. In fact, at one point, I actually said, "Well, I'm the teacher and I know education. This is the best course of action." (I know, I know. Bad move.)

She responded with, "Well, I'm his mother. You may know education, but I know my son."

Needless to say, we didn't get on the same page that day. Not only did I lose the argument, I lost her support. It was a long remainder of the year.

It is vital to work with parents instead of arguing with them. They *do* know their children better than you do, and they do have ideas about how to best deal with their children. Rather than insist that your way is the best way, shift the conversation to focus on considering what will be best for the student. Don't argue about strategies; discuss the effect of your way or their way, and work together to figure out which effect will make the biggest difference for the student.

ADMIT WHEN YOU'RE WRONG

When a parent is coming to see you about an error you've made, it's tempting to cover your mistakes. After all, if parents see that you have made a mistake, they may no longer trust you. And some parents can point out our errors in such a nasty way that it often feels better to just deny, deny, deny rather than give in to their goading and possibly set yourself up for further harassment. Besides, it's just plain embarrassing to be wrong.

But hiding your mistakes can actually make things worse. I know. For years, I carefully covered my mistakes with parents. Even when I was wrong, I held to my stance because I thought that to admit a mistake to a parent was to admit weakness and give parents the upper hand. Sometimes, I'd even quietly make amends, but I always did so under the guise of being benevolent, never admitting any wrongdoing.

At the time I thought I was doing the right thing. Even my colleagues and supervisors encouraged me to cover myself and never admit my mistakes. But it didn't feel right.

During my third year of teaching, I finally found the courage to own up to a mistake I'd made with a parent. It wasn't a clear mistake; I could have justifiably covered it up. I had a grading policy that made sense and worked in most situations. However, in this instance my policy penalized a student unfairly. My impulse was to stick with my policy. After all, if I let a parent talk me into making an exception for his daughter, then it would just open the floodgates of appeals from other parents. It was unfortunate that this student would suffer, but in the end, it was better that one student suffer rather than open the door to an onslaught of other appeals, I reasoned. But all the while, there was a voice in the back of my head that nagged me: *Am I in the business of protecting policy or protecting students?*

This voice wouldn't let me rest. The next afternoon, I met with the father at his request to go over the grading policy. The father had prepared well and made a reasoned argument for why the policy had been unfair to his daughter. The more I listened, the more I became convinced of his point. Still, I didn't want to budge. I felt it would show weakness.

At first, I desperately tried to figure out a way to still be "right" and yet make the reasonable concessions he offered. I didn't want him to think he'd "won." But there was no way around it. Finally, I admitted, "Sir, I see your point." Then I offered a resolution that incorporated his concessions—but I didn't stop there. I also made a few suggestions so that we wouldn't end up in the same situation again. We agreed on a plan of action, and I adjusted my policy for all of my students to correct the mistake the father had pointed out. Rather than feeling weak, I felt that the father had actually helped me become a better teacher.

DON'T TRY TO DEFUSE; LISTEN

Some parents are so frustrated that they just need to talk. The moment you try to defuse their anger, they feel like you are just "handling" them, and they get even more frustrated and angry. I've learned that the best way to deal with a parent like this is to just listen.

It wasn't always that way. I remember getting advice that if a parent was yelling, I was to interrupt them and tell them that I would not be spoken to that way and then leave.

While I still believe in this advice if I feel that I am in danger, I've found that it doesn't work when I have a parent who is fed up but not threatening. In fact, it could make them *more* frustrated and angry.

I actually didn't learn this lesson until I became an administrator. As a teacher, I would get stomachaches every time I had to meet with an angry parent. I was so terrified that I would end up overpreparing for the meeting and be more focused on defending myself than I was on doing what was best for the student. But as an administrator, my role was to talk to angry parents all the time and try to come to a solution that protected my teachers and did what was best for my students. My defensiveness wasn't going to work.

I remember the first time I had to deal with an angry parent as an administrator. The other administrators were terrified of this parent, as were the teachers. It was my first month as an administrator and I really didn't know what I was doing. The parent's child was in our program for students with emotional challenges and had a history of violence with the staff. We had gotten him placed in another school that was better equipped to meet his needs, but we were waiting for the paperwork to go through so that we could transfer him. One Friday afternoon, the student had left class and was running around the building. The staff had tried to get him back to class, but to no avail. Given the student's history, his case worker suggested that we call his father rather than put him in a restraint. I was the only administrator in the building, so I had to make the call.

Nervously, I dialed his number. I had been apprised of his history of being verbally abusive to staff, so I was bracing myself for an onslaught. And boy, did I get it. He yelled. He screamed. He called me names. He threatened to sue the school. For fifteen minutes he raged, and I listened.

When he finally ran out of steam, I remained quiet on the line for a few moments, stunned by his vitriol. Finally, he broke the silence.

"Wow. You're a really good listener," he said.

"Thank you," I replied because I really didn't know what else to say.

"I'll come up and pick up my son. I'll be there in twenty minutes."

Those were some of the longest twenty minutes of my career. We were all nervous about what the father would do once he got there. When he finally did arrive, I went out front to greet him. He was downright jovial. He shook my hand, walked with me to collect his son, and they both came into my office. He thanked me again for listening to him and apologized for screaming at me. He told me how frustrated he was with the school system and how no one listened to him anymore. Then he thanked me and left.

The other teachers were flabbergasted. They had never seen this father so polite, calm, and nice. From that day to this, I have found that with some parents, you just have to hear them out. I don't try to calm them down or cajole them. I listen.

> *Let them get out what's on their minds. You don't have to fix it. You don't even have to agree. But hear them out.*

Instead of trying to manage these parents, let them get out what's on their minds. You don't have to fix it. You don't even have to agree. But hear them out. It can go a long way toward defusing their frustration and anger and getting them to the point where they can hear what you have to say and cooperate.

SOME PARENTS WON'T WANT TO GET INVOLVED, AND THAT'S OKAY

I have called parents and had them yell at me for interrupting them at work. I have begged parents to get involved only to have them tell me that I should handle school and they will handle home. At first, I judged those parents. I thought that they didn't care enough about their students. But judging got me nowhere.

Finally, I asked myself why I wanted parents to get involved. Mostly, I wanted their support to reinforce what I was teaching students at school. If I couldn't get that from the parents, I wondered, how else could I get that support?

After thinking about it for a while, I realized that if I couldn't get the support I needed from parents at home, I would have to find a way to provide that support at school. So I found ways to ensure that my students didn't suffer from a lack of parental support by finding ways to provide the support I felt they needed during the school day.

Not every parent will be involved, for a myriad of reasons. Some parents want to be involved but work and life demands prevent them. Other parents don't know how to get involved. Still others have had such a limited school experience themselves or have had such a bad school experience that they avoid getting involved. Rather than lament the fact that parents aren't involved, look for ways to supplement parental involvement to accomplish what you want to accomplish with your students. For instance, a lot of students need help from parents to do their homework. If they can't get that support at home, how can you give it to them at school? You could set up homework clubs and invite volunteers to help students with their homework before and after school, or you could use a flipped approach to instruction. Ask yourself why you need parental support, and look for ways to supplement it at school.

DON'T BE A TATTLETALE

When you're frustrated with a student, it's easy to fall into the trap of wanting to tell on him to his mother, with the hopes that perhaps his mother can make him do what you can't.

Don't.

If parents think that you cannot control their child, they will not support you. I learned this lesson the hard way. I had a student once who was so disruptive, so disrespectful, that I dreaded seeing him each day and rejoiced on the days that he was absent. I was at my wit's end as to how to make him behave, so I called his father. During the first phone call, I described his behavior and asked the father for help working with his son at home. The father was cooperative and agreed to speak with his son. His son's behavior improved for a couple of days, but by week's end, he was back to his old tricks. So I called the father again. Again, he agreed to talk to his son, and his son's behavior improved. For a while.

When the son began to act up again, I called the father again. And again. And again. He soon tired of my "wait 'til you hear what Johnny did at school today" calls and exploded, "Look, Ms. Jackson. I can't do my job and your job too. If you cannot figure out how to control my son, maybe you ought not be a teacher!" and then he hung up.

I sat there stunned. I'll admit that I was furious too. I even began to blame him. It isn't *my* fault that he raised such a brat, I railed. But beneath my indignation was the nagging feeling that there was some truth to what he said.

I had stopped trying to manage that student's behavior and instead would just run and tell his daddy every time he misbehaved. That couldn't be my only classroom management technique.

> *If I had asked the father what he was doing at home that had worked with his son instead of tattling, I could have learned something.*

The problem was that I didn't know how to manage that student. I had a limited number of strategies, and none of them worked with him. I realized that if I had asked the father what he was doing at home that had worked with his son instead of tattling, I could have learned something. Since that line of communication was now closed, I went to the student's other teachers and asked them what worked for them. I tried a few of their suggestions and had a little success. Then I called his father to report the progress his son was making. You could hear the relief in the father's voice. Every parent wants to hear that his child is a good kid. The father thanked me profusely for the call, and that call reopened the lines of communication. His son didn't miraculously become an angel after that. It was still a struggle managing him, but I learned an important lesson: Tattling on kids to their parents doesn't work.

It was several years before I developed a formula for sharing bad news with parents that does work. Instead of calling parents to tattle, I call parents and use the following process:

1. **Give them the news—along with your plan.** I start by sharing with parents their child's behavior and my plan for addressing and correcting that behavior in the classroom. I also give parents a chance to react to my plan.

2. **Ask for input.** Next I ask parents for any insight they may have about what works with their child at home. I want to know if there is a way to make my plan of action better. This gives parents a chance to talk about their process for dealing with their students and gives me rich information that can round out my approach with their child.

3. **Enlist help, and be specific.** Finally, I ask parents for specific things they can do to support my course of action and reinforce it at home. Perhaps I need them to enforce a homework hour at home or to check the student's notebook each day. Giving parents specific ways to support what is happening in the classroom secures parents' cooperation and makes us a united front.

4. **End the call with something good.** Before the call is over, I make sure to convey to the parent something positive about their child. I want parents to know that I like their child and that I am invested in their child's

success. Ending on a positive note makes it more likely that you will sustain parental support over time.

I have found that when I call this way, the conversations are always productive. Parents appreciate being made partners and usually support my plan.

DON'T GANG UP ON STUDENTS

Sometimes, parents are not fighting against us. Sometimes they are right on our side and willing to do whatever we ask. While that may feel good, be careful. When all the adults are on the same side, it can be overwhelming to the student, especially if we and the parents are similarly frustrated with the student. Without intending to, we can gang up on him.

I remember being in one parent conference with a student who had stopped doing her work in school. Her parents were at their wits' end, and so were all of her teachers. We gathered together in the room for a parent conference, but it quickly turned into an "intervention," with all the adults in the room pleading with the student to turn herself around and become the sweet child she once was. At one point, I turned to the student, who was seated to my left, and looked directly into her eyes and told her that everyone in that room wanted the best for her. As I spoke passionately about how much we all cared about her, I could see her shutting down. She maintained eye contact with me throughout my speech, but it was as if she had pulled down the blinds behind her eyes. She wasn't there.

I'd never seen anything like it. As others began to talk, I continued to watch her. She had shut us all out, but I couldn't figure out why. We weren't yelling at her or berating her. We were gathered to help her.

I didn't realize it then, but I have come to learn that sometimes even when we're helping it can look like we're ganging up on the student. Here were all the authority figures in her life together at one time in perfect harmony, and it was very overwhelming for her. She had nowhere to run. What if we had prepared her for the conference instead? What if we had empowered her to speak and had shown her how to advocate for herself? What if we had made her a partner in her own education?

When working with parents, we need to be careful not to gang up on the student. The best way to do this is to make sure the student feels supported and convey the idea that all of the adults are working together in the best interest of the student.

DON'T FIGHT IN FRONT OF THE CHILDREN

There will be times when parents will disagree with you in the meeting. If we're not careful, we can put students in the really uncomfortable position of having to mediate between all the adults in the room. They may feel that they have to choose sides between their parents and their teacher. In the end, no matter what side he chooses, the student always loses.

Once, I gave a student detention and called his father at the end of the school day to tell him. I was in the middle of explaining why I was assigning detention when he interrupted, "How dare you! I'm coming down there right now to straighten this out and you better be there when I get there!" He hung up.

I quickly told my principal what happened and waited for the father to show up. Twenty minutes later, he stormed in the main office and insisted on speaking to me. The office staff paged me and I came down filled with dread. The father was pacing angrily in the lobby with his son. I swallowed hard and invited him to the main office conference room to talk. Because I was afraid of what might happen, I invited one of the assistant principals to join us.

As soon as he was seated, the father started in on me. He told me that I had been harassing his son the entire year and he was sick of it.

"But Dad…," his son tried to interrupt.

"Let me handle this!" his father snapped and then launched back into his rant. "My son will *not* be serving your little detention and that is final," he ended dramatically. As hard as it was to sit there and listen to his tirade, I noticed that it was even harder on his son. He seemed embarrassed and terribly uncomfortable being there.

"Sir, would you please ask your son to wait outside?" I asked.

"What for?" he countered. "He has every right to be here."

"Of course he has," I agreed. "But why don't we work this out between the two of us? He doesn't need to hear all of this." I turned to his son. "Sweetheart, why don't you let your dad and me talk for a bit and you can wait outside?"

"Don't you tell him what to do," the father yelled.

"Okay," I demurred. "Then why don't you ask him to wait outside?"

The father looked at me for a moment and then turned to his son, "Go outside and wait until we're finished here."

Once his son was outside, I turned to the father. "You love your son very much," I began.

"Yes I do, and I'm not going to let anyone mistreat him!" He pounded the conference table.

"What do you hope for your son? What kind of person do you hope he becomes?" I asked.

He explained the values he hoped his son would espouse and the kind of man he wanted his son to be one day. I listened quietly.

When he finished, I asked, "How does getting him out of this detention help him become that kind of man? He admits that he did wrong. If you don't allow him to experience this consequence, what lesson does he learn? What kind of man will he become?"

The father sat quietly and stared at his hands. "Sir," I continued. "I am not trying to punish your son. I simply want to allow him to experience the consequences of his actions so that he can learn from them and become the kind of man you just described."

The room was silent for a long time. Finally, the father said, "Okay. I will allow him to do your detention."

"Thank you," I nodded. I saw how hard it was for the father to make this concession, especially after the bluster he came into the meeting with. He needed a way to save face with his son. "Now, before we bring your son back in, let's talk about how we tell him. I think you should tell him that he will do the detention and explain why. He should hear it from you."

I got up and called his son back into the office. He looked terrified. Once he sat down, his father haltingly explained that he had decided that his son should do the detention and explained why. Rather than look disappointed, his son actually looked relieved. Sure, he didn't want to do the detention, but at least the adults were no longer fighting. We were on the same page.

You've surely heard parent horror stories, and if you're new to teaching you're probably a little intimidated when it comes to dealing with parents. You may even feel a little under attack when they call or contact you to discuss their children. But remember, parents are your partners. You both want what is best for the student, even when you cannot agree on what "best" is at the moment.

And even when parents are rude, disrespectful, inappropriate, or just downright nasty, I try to keep my focus on the student. That doesn't mean that I allow myself to be abused—you shouldn't either. But it does mean that I don't take parents' bad behavior personally. I keep my focus on what is best for the student.

The truth is, I've found most parents to be supportive and eager to do whatever it takes to help their children be successful, and you will find that as well. Parents can be your best allies and your biggest fans if you love and nurture their children. Remember, they are entrusting us with what they value most—their children. This is a sacred trust, and if you take it seriously and keep your focus on what's best for students, you can work with parents successfully.

CHAPTER 6

YOU CAN KEEP THINGS RUNNING SMOOTHLY
MANAGING YOUR CLASSROOM

In my early years of teaching, I thought that classroom management was all about maintaining control over my classroom. I focused exclusively on running a tight ship. I didn't want anyone to accuse me of not having my students under control. The thing they don't tell you about classroom management is that it is as much about managing yourself as it is about managing your students. So rather than spend time telling you a bunch of classroom management tricks that you can probably read in other books, in this chapter, I want to share with you a few things they might not have told you about how to manage your classroom effectively. Hopefully, these little nuances will make a world of difference as you try to manage your own classroom.

SOMETIMES, *YOU'RE* THE DISCIPLINE PROBLEM

One of the most enlightening things I have ever learned about classroom management is the difference between a discipline problem and a motivation problem. "A discipline problem is behavior that (1) interferes with the teaching act; (2) interferes with the rights of others to learn; (3) is psychologically or physically unsafe; or (4) destroys property" (Levin & Nolan, 1996, p. 22). A motivation problem, on the other hand, is a student's decision not to invest in the classroom or his or her own learning. These are two very different things.

One of the biggest mistakes we can make is to confuse the two. The strategies that work to address discipline problems are not the same ones needed to deal with motivational issues and vice versa. Once I learned the distinction between the two, I also learned two valuable lessons about discipline.

The first is that, based on the definition of a discipline problem, the teacher could be the problem. If we use classroom management techniques inappropriately or ineffectively, if our lessons are not planned carefully, if our classroom procedures are not firmly established or are inconsistently applied, we can disrupt the teaching and learning process and become a discipline problem.

I thought that dis-
cipline problems were
something exclusive to
my students; but after
some careful reflec-
tion, I realized that
there were times when

> *Classroom manage-ment techniques only work to solve discipline problems; they don't work to address motivation problems.*

I was indeed the problem. I remember one time in particular when my class was supposed to be reading silently. I
noticed that one student didn't have her book out. I marched
over to her desk and told her to take her book out and start
reading. She said that she didn't have her book. I began to
fuss at her so loudly that I not only escalated the situation
between her and me, I also distracted the students who
were reading. Her not having her book out was not a discipline problem. My frustrated response to her not having
her book out became one.

That brings me to the second lesson I learned: Classroom management techniques only work to solve discipline problems; they don't work to address motivation
problems. That means that it is important to understand
the nature of the problem before jumping to a solution. My
student who didn't have her book was actually exhibiting
a motivation problem, not a discipline problem. Before I
knew the distinction, I treated motivation problems as discipline problems and used rewards, punishments, logical

consequences, and carrots and sticks to try to deal with persistent and seemingly intractable student resistance. It never worked because I was using the wrong strategies to address the wrong problems. Once I understood the difference, I was able to develop the right tools for the right problems, and that made a huge difference.

So, take time to determine first whether you're dealing with a discipline problem or a motivation problem. It's the best way to be sure that how you address the problem doesn't create an additional discipline problem in your classroom.

REMEMBER, YOU'RE NOT THEIR PEERS

When I first started teaching, I taught high school juniors and seniors, which meant that I was only about five years older than most of my students. I looked younger than most of them. At first, it was really hard for me to establish authority. It wasn't that the students didn't accept my authority as the teacher; *I* had a hard time accepting my own authority.

I was young. I still wanted to be hip and cool. When I wasn't in school, I dressed like my students, listened to the same music, watched some of the same television shows. Sometimes they would come into class discussing some movie or item of celebrity gossip and I had to bite my tongue not to join in the conversation as a peer instead of their teacher. It was hard being the adult.

I tried to remember that feeling several years later when I supervised a group of new teachers. One of them, a brand-new middle school teacher, would come to work dressed in jeans, tee shirts, and flip flops every day. We tried to tell her as best we could that she needed to dress more formally, but she told us that "these are the clothes that I can afford." My colleagues and I suggested that she buy just a few key pieces, or that she visit a consignment shop, or at least that she wear shirts that cover her rear end, but she told us that we were being too old-fashioned. After a few months of teaching, however. she started to notice that the boys in her class would snicker every time she wrote on the board. And her interactions with the girls in her class were sometimes tinged with resentment. She couldn't understand what was happening until one day she learned the problem. It seems that when she reached to write on the board, her shirt would rise up and reveal the top of her thong.

Another teacher I once worked with complained that her students treated her with little respect. On the day she mentioned this to me she was wearing fuzzy slippers because they were "more comfortable" than regular shoes for standing all day. I pointed to her footwear and gently suggested, "Perhaps if you dressed a little differently, students would take you more seriously."

She immediately got offended. "What does how I choose to dress have to do with it?" she snapped.

Frankly, a whole lot.

I'm going to sound a little like an old fogey here, but hear me out. No matter what grade you teach, what you wear conveys a certain sense of authority. This isn't just my old-fashioned sensibilities talking here. It really does make a difference. Every career has a uniform. If you were an attorney, you'd put a suit on for court. If you were a chef, you'd wear the jacket and toque. If you were a regional sales manager, you'd dust off your power suit to meet important clients. Even I wear a uniform when I lead presentations.

So think carefully about your teacher uniform. If you teach younger students, you don't need to wear a power suit each day. But you do need to wear clothing that is modest, that fits, and that can take a glue stain or two. And while you're at it, check yourself from all angles to make sure that your underwear doesn't show when you bend over. If you teach older students, find something other than jeans to wear to work. Even if you switch to khakis, it will be a huge differentia-tor between you and your students, and that really is the point. You *You need to look different from your students.* need to look different from your students.

Not only does how you dress convey authority, how you speak and write goes a long way toward establishing respect with your students and their parents. You may text in real life, but when you communicate with students and parents, use more formal language. That means no LOLs at the end of e-mails to parents and no OMGs when responding to students' work. IJS. Assuming a more formal tone in your written and verbal communication will establish gravitas with parents and boundaries with students.

And boundaries are indeed important if you want to maintain discipline in your classroom. I once met a first-grade teacher who would invite her female students to her house on the weekend for slumber parties. She would stay up all night and do their hair and cook them breakfast the next morning. They adored her, and she loved being the "cool" teacher. But she got caught up in the politics of the various first-grade girl cliques and began to favor some of the girls over others. Soon not everyone was getting an invitation to her house on the weekends. After a while, she became no different from one of the "mean girls." The "in" girls started taking liberties at school that they were given at the weekend slumber parties, and the other students took notice. Soon, she was experiencing mini-mutinies in the classroom and angry phone calls from parents.

Another teacher I worked with was very handsome in a "rebel poet" kind of way. He taught English at a local high school, and the teenage girls thought he was just dreamy. At first he deflected their admiration, but he started running into them on the weekends at the same clubs, the same coffee houses, and the same concerts he attended with his friends. Sometimes he would strike up casual conversations with them, but soon those conversations turned to text messages. After a while, his students began to treat him more like a friend than a teacher. Although we warned him about the importance of boundaries, he told us that we were being too uptight and that the connections he made with students off campus were actually helping him reach his students in class. But the problem with letting boundaries slip is that at some point, you end up crossing the line.

You may think I am being dramatic here, but these stories continue to repeat themselves, over and over again. The first and most important step to establishing good discipline is to establish good boundaries.

YOU'RE NOT THEIR PARENTS OR THEIR COLLEAGUES, EITHER

Not everyone comes to teaching fresh out of school. Some of you have come to the profession after having careers outside of education. So while you are clear that you're not your students' peers, you may face the opposite challenge: What worked for you as a parent, a grandparent, or even a colleague in your former career may not work for you in the classroom.

Often when I work with new teachers who are coming to teaching after rearing their own children, I see them attempt to parent their students. They try to use the same techniques they used with their own children and cannot understand why those strategies don't work. But parenting is fundamentally different from teaching, and what works at home with your own children will often fail miserably in the classroom (and vice versa).

Other times, I have seen new teachers who enjoyed successful careers outside of education attempt to manage their classrooms the same way that they managed their offices or supervised their staff. They expect students to exhibit the same respectful behavior they've come to expect in the workplace. Such expectations are bound to lead to disappointment, and after a few weeks in the classroom, these teachers are often appalled by their students' behavior and incredulous that schools don't work the same way as businesses.

One teacher I coached was brand new to teaching even though she had successfully run her own business for years. She was in her late fifties and thought that by going into teaching, she could give back and help young people gain a leg up in life. So she enrolled in a master's of teaching program and spent two years learning how to become a teacher. She was a good student, earned excellent grades, and was lauded by her professors. She thought she was ready to teach.

But shortly after landing a classroom of her own, she began to flounder. She had beautifully written lesson plans, a carefully organized classroom, and an arsenal of teaching strategies, and yet she could not get her frisky fourth graders to settle down and learn. By the time I met her, she was completely bewildered. She was doing everything "right" and applying every piece of feedback she received from her principal or instructional coach, using every effective strategy she learned at a workshop or read in journal articles, and doing everything exactly by the book. She was bewildered as to why none of it was working for her.

After observing her classroom and speaking with her afterward, I figured out her problem. She was approaching teaching using the same strategies that made her a successful businesswoman: She researched best practices, applied them to her classroom, and waited for them to work. Not only that, she was managing her classroom in the same way that she managed her staff. But as she had to learn, fourth graders are very different from employees; it would take a completely different approach to manage them.

Classroom management is unlike anything you've ever done before in your life. It takes an entirely different skill set. While your life experience is a real advantage in that it makes you well-rounded and provides you with a marvelous perspective, it will not prepare you for what it's like to facilitate and manage a learning experience for dozens of students. You come to teaching with a range of experiences that can be a real asset in the classroom. Your challenge will be to bring your experience to bear while also remaining open to an entirely different way of thinking about and seeing your work.

REMEMBER, YOU'RE THERE TO TEACH, NOT TO CONTROL

The purpose of discipline is not to get control over your class or your students. Your job is not to make them behave. Your job is to help them learn, and you cannot do that unless there is order in the classroom.

The difference between controlling your classroom and managing it is a fine distinction but an important one. Control puts all the onus on you. You have to get students to do the things you want them to do or keep them from doing something you don't want them to do.

Management is different. It's a partnership. You create an environment that is best suited for learning, and you help students choose to do those things that will best facilitate their learning. Your job isn't to control students' behavior. Your job is to do those things that best help them learn and ultimately teach them how to manage their own behavior.

One of the hardest aspects of classroom management is teaching students how to manage their own behavior. It is much easier to simply control the classroom yourself through your rules, rewards, and punishments. A lot of teachers spend their entire careers managing their classrooms this way, and, on the surface, it looks as if their classrooms are organized, their students are on task, and learning is happening in the classroom.

But the moment that teacher lets up, the moment that teacher turns her back, what do her students do? They resort back to the behaviors they've been suppressing. So while managing student behavior has many short-term benefits, it isn't as effective as helping students learn how to manage themselves. When students manage their own behavior, they'll do the right thing whether you're watching or not.

If you see classroom management as being about control, you'll resort to coercive techniques in order to maintain that control. If, however, you see classroom management as about helping students learn how to manage their own behavior, every disciplinary incident becomes a real opportunity to teach. It makes a big difference in how you will ultimately deal with students.

NEVER EMBARRASS YOUR STUDENTS

Recently I was observing a class of a fairly new teacher and what I saw made me both angry and deeply sad. He was teaching a math lesson and had become frustrated because some of his students weren't really understanding the concept. He kept admonishing them to pay more attention, but some of the students who were struggling the most were, in fact, paying attention and they still weren't getting it. Another student who had tried to understand the problem earlier in the class period had finally given up and adopted an "I-don't-care" attitude, and then started distracting other students. Finally the teacher got so frustrated by the student who wasn't paying attention that he moved her desk away from the others and reprimanded her, "This is why you are still not understanding. If you paid attention, you would get this."

She rolled her eyes and began to doodle on her paper. He went back to explaining. About three minutes later, another student gave the wrong answer and he stopped and looked at her incredulously. "You really think it's 'y'?" he asked.

She slunk down in her seat and shrugged.

The teacher turned to another struggling student and asked, "Do you think the answer is 'y,' too?"

That student shrugged. The teacher walked to the front of the room and said, "Thumbs up if you think it's 'x,' thumbs down if you think it's 'y,' and thumbs sideways if you don't know."

The students responded by placing their thumbs in the air. Three students had their thumbs sideways. The teacher scanned the class and noticed that the student whom he had moved away from the others had her thumb sideways. He rolled his eyes.

"Okay, everyone who has their thumb sideways stand up," he commanded. Three students stood. "Okay, everyone who is sitting down, give yourself 10 points." The seated students wrote 10 points on their papers. The standing students stood hanging their heads. Then the teacher chastised the standing students. "The reason that you don't know whether it's 'x' or 'y' is because you're not paying attention. You need to pay more attention. Now sit down." The students slunk back into their seats and stared at their papers. The teacher moved on.

I sat there frozen and seething inside. He didn't see it, but I saw how he had just broken his students' spirits. He thought he was making a point, but all he was doing was making them feel stupid. He never checked back to see whether the students had gotten it, and I can tell you from where I was sitting that they never did.

Perhaps right now you are as appalled and outraged hearing about this classroom as I was witnessing it, but this teacher is not alone. If I'm honest, I have gotten so frustrated with a student that I have done things that have embarrassed them or shamed them or made them feel stupid. I forgot sometimes that I was the teacher and acted just as badly as my students.

One of my biggest disciplinary mistakes was that I took everything personally. If the students disobeyed me, I got angry at them. If they didn't do their work, I took it as a personal affront. If they put their heads on their desks, I thought it impugned the quality of my lectures. Of course,

now I know that it's
probably not personal.
It seldom is. There are
a lot of reasons stu-
dents disobey, or don't
do their work, or sleep
during class, and very

> *Many times your
> frustration will be justified.
> But your frustration is never
> —let me repeat that—never a
> reason to embarrass students.*

few of them have to do with the teacher. When I finally
learned not to take things personally, I was able to shift my
focus from how offended I was to what I needed to do to
help my students make better decisions next time.

You will get frustrated with students, and many times
your frustration will be justified. But your frustration is
never—let me repeat that—*never* a reason to embarrass
students. We have the power to help students, but we also
have the power to irrevocably harm them if we are not
careful. One moment of frustration from us, one bad move
on our part, and we could damage them for life. So be
careful. Be very careful that you don't lose it.

~~~

Classroom management is perhaps the hardest part of
teaching, especially when you are new. It takes time to
establish yourself and figure out what will work best for
you. The tricks and strategies that you learned in school
may or may not work, and figuring out the right combination of techniques to use is in many ways a matter of trial

and error. What's even more challenging is that what may work on one student may not work for another.

I am not telling you this to depress or discourage you; I'm telling you this so that you won't have unrealistic expectations about your first few years of teaching. All of us struggle with classroom management at the beginning. All of us have to figure out what works for us, and all of us have to readjust our classroom management strategies throughout our career as we have different classes or combinations of students who need different support. It is an ongoing process.

There are several great books on classroom management out there, and I encourage you to read them. They contain some really useful strategies that you can add to your repertoire. But I warn you not to see any strategy as a magic bullet. You have to figure out what will work for you, and it may take a while before you can make everything you've learned work for you and your students. Be gentle on yourself and know that even if you don't get it right the first time or even the tenth time, students are forgiving. You can always start again.

REFERENCE

Levin, J. & Nolan, J. (1996) *Principles of Classroom Management*, Second Edition. Boston: Allyn and Bacon.

CHAPTER 7

YOU CAN BOUNCE BACK
RECOVERING FROM MISTAKES

I'm going to tell you one of the most embarrassing things that ever happened to me as a teacher, but only if you promise not to laugh.

Early in my teaching career, I had a class of twenty-three boys and five girls. Right after lunch. Not only that, I didn't have a classroom of my own and had to teach from a cart I wheeled around to various classrooms around the building. The classroom that I used for this particular class belonged to a colleague who had decorated her classroom to feel more like a living space, preferring to use lamplight rather than the harsh overhead florescent lights of the classroom, and hanging art on the walls rather than the typical teacher posters. It was a lovely space, to be sure, but her efforts at homeness were lost on this particular group of students, who saw all of her nice touches as invitations to mischief.

Getting the class started was a challenge. Because students were allowed to leave campus for lunch, many of my students had trouble getting back to school on time for class. They tended to trickle in five to ten minutes after the bell. Getting them settled and working was another challenge. The last thing they were interested in was parsing sentences or finding out whether Elizabeth actually ends up with Mr. Darcy. They started class with loads of energy because they had just finished lunch, but by the end of the class period, once the sugar high subsided, most of them were fast asleep.

I tried everything. I mean I pulled out my best stuff. I tried to engage them in interesting discussions, but all too often, what started out as an intellectual examination of Othello's motivation ended up as a raunchy discussion of his sex life, no matter how hard I worked to keep things on track. I tried cooperative learning activities to keep students actively engaged in their work but quickly found that they were more interested in teasing each other than they were in completing the assignment. I even went down to the guidance department and tried to have two or three of my most difficult students transferred to other periods or even other teachers, thinking that if I could just break up the group a little by removing some of the ringleaders, perhaps I could get the class on track. Nothing worked.

Well, I won't say nothing worked. The only thing that *did* work was lots and lots of worksheets. That seemed to be the only thing that would get my students settled and working. Although my teaching style was more geared to active student participation, and I was suspicious of teachers who gave nothing but worksheets, I was quickly becoming one of those teachers. Worksheets, as much as I distrusted them, were my most effective classroom management tool.

The other four or five periods of the day, I taught with lots of active discussions that challenged my students to think and interesting teaching activities that deepened their thinking. Four out of five periods of the day, I was the teacher I aspired to be. But every day during fifth period, I became the teacher I dreaded: I passed out worksheets.

As ashamed as I am to admit that I relied on worksheets as a classroom management technique, that's not the embarrassing part. One day as my students were completing yet another worksheet, I was helping one student with a particular question when I heard a commotion behind me. I turned around to see one of the lamps on fire.

I stood there stunned for a moment as flames leaped from the lamp. The boys who had set the lamp on fire were leaping from their seats and quickly moving away from the flames, while the other students sat silently fascinated by the impressively growing fire. One of the girls in the classroom screamed, and smoke began to fill the

I just stood there watching the lamp—and my teaching career—go up in flames.

classroom. I just stood there watching the lamp—and my teaching career—go up in flames.

One of the boys nearest the lamp grabbed his jacket and began to beat at the flames. The lamp crashed to the floor, and he stomped on it. Another boy took the soda he had snuck into the classroom and dumped it on the lamp. Between the beating, stomping, and dumping, the flames finally went out and left a sticky mass of burned metal, glass, ashes and orange soda on the floor.

The silence that followed was deafening as the students waited for my reaction. I stood there staring at the lamp, as it slowly occurred to me what had just happened. *My students had set my classroom on fire.* My principal was going to kill me. Their parents would kill me. Judy, whose classroom we were sharing, was going to kill me. What kind of teacher allows her students to set the classroom on fire?

The stench was putrid, and I coughed slightly at the smoke. Somehow I found my voice and quietly asked what happened. My students were too stunned to lie. Two boys admitted that they were playing an impromptu game of basketball by tossing paper into the top of the lamp when it suddenly caught on fire.

"Please take your things and go wait for me in the main office," I instructed. I turned to another student, "Go find Mr. Flores (our school custodian) and tell him that we've had an accident." I turned to the rest of the class, "Move your desks over to this side of the room and open a few windows." My students began to move warily, watching me as they did. They knew that they had gone too far and seemed to be waiting for me to explode. I wanted to explode. I really did. But I was too terrified, too afraid that my teaching career was over, to do much more than get them back to work while I mentally reviewed what would happen next. The principal would call me into his office. He'd yell at me for endangering children, order me to pack my things, and have security escort me out of the building. I'd be blackballed, never allowed to teach again. There might even be an article about me in the local paper: "Bad Teacher Allows Students to Set Her Classroom on Fire." I'd end up working at McDonald's, but only working the counter because no one in their right mind would let me anywhere near the stove.

This was my first big mistake as a teacher, but it wasn't my last. It took me a while (and several more mistakes) before I learned this: *You will make mistakes. Accept it. There's no way around it.* You will make mistakes. But as you'll learn, mistakes are often the best teachers if you allow yourself to learn from them. Here are several ways that you can transform mistakes into your best teachers:

ADMIT YOU MADE A MISTAKE

For many years of my teaching career, I was afraid to make mistakes. I thought that as the teacher, I always had to be right. I worked really hard at being the smartest person in the room. When my students asked me a question for which I had no answer, I'd make one up. If I made a mistake, I would cover it up. Only when I learned to relax did my teaching get really good. When I let my students see me make mistakes, admit them, and then take steps to correct them, it made it okay for them to make mistakes too. The more I took risks in the classroom, the more I made it safe for them to take risks. As a result, my classroom became a place where real learning could take place.

One of my good friends once told me of how he learned from his mistakes. It was his first year of teaching, and he wanted desperately to be an amazing teacher. He planned all summer and was eager to start the year. But his first classes were disasters. His carefully planned lessons fell apart in the face of thirty-two very active seventh graders who couldn't have cared less about his carefully constructed science labs and preferred to have mock sword fights with the meter sticks instead. His dreams of being a master teacher quickly fell apart as his classes got worse and worse and worse. He realized that what he was doing wasn't working, but he felt trapped by the structures and rules he had set up at the beginning of the year. He thought that he couldn't change.

Finally, one Friday, he got so frustrated with the class structure that was clearly not working that he couldn't take it anymore. That weekend, he went home and redesigned his science labs to provide more structure while keeping students engaged.

That Monday, he started his class by telling his students that what they were doing clearly wasn't working. He then laid out the new rules and procedures for science labs. To his surprise, his students quickly got on board, and his classroom was transformed for the better. He told me later, "If I had never taken the risk and revamped things, I would have been stuck with that awful class all year long. I'm glad I did it. It changed everything, and it taught me that you can always redirect."

It's advice that he still gives new teachers to this day. You can *always* start again. If something isn't working, you don't have to be stuck with it. You can redirect, change, refocus. You can always start again.

I've done it countless times, sometimes even in the middle of the lesson. When I see that something isn't working, I change course. I redirect. Lessons fall flat. Plans don't work out. Rules that seem like a good idea on paper don't turn out to make sense. When your horse dies, dismount. Don't tie yourself to strategies that you know aren't working. Redirect. Start over. Try again.

You're allowed.

LEARN THE *RIGHT* WAY TO FAIL

Some failure is inevitable, and as much as we all hate to fail, it's one of the most powerful ways to learn as an educator. In fact, whenever I talk to master teachers and ask them when they felt that they finally achieved mastery, it was usually just after a huge failure. What they learned from that failure filled in something missing from their practice, helped them cross the line from good to great, and ultimately made them a master teacher.

For me, that moment came when I finally realized that although I was really effective with a certain kind of student, I was failing with others. It had to do with the kind of feedback I gave my students. As an English teacher, I took a lot of time writing what I thought were helpful comments on students' papers. I studied strategies for writing coaching comments, was very careful to offer one or, at the most, two final pointers to give my students focus, and tried very hard to get at the root cause of my students' writing difficulties. And yet, my students weren't getting any better. Most ignored my comments. Others tried to address my comments but ended up making their next paper worse. Only a few used my comments to improve.

At first, I blamed my students. I fussed at them for ignoring my comments on their papers or silently fumed when they made the same mistakes over and over again. I wrote fewer comments or more comments or no comments at all. I sat with students and reviewed my comments with them. I even made them rewrite my comments on a goal sheet and explain how they addressed each one in their rewrites. Nothing worked.

I knew that I was failing these kids, but it took me a long time to admit that maybe my comments were the problem. It was easier to blame the kids or to look for a better solution, rather than examine why my process was failing.

I still remember the moment I admitted defeat. I was sitting in a faculty meeting trying to secretly catch up on my grading. I had just read a student's paper and was silently seething that in spite of all of my comments and targeting instruction, the student continued to make the same mistakes over and over. I remember putting the paper down on the cafeteria table and staring at the soda machine in front of me. *I'm failing to help these students become better writers*, I finally admitted to myself. It felt awful. I didn't know what to do. If I couldn't help them become better writers, then I was failing them and failing at teaching. I wanted to cry.

But here's the difference between simply failing and "failing up." As awful as I felt, I reminded myself of something that I had recently started telling my students: Anyone can get better at anything with the right kind of effort. In my case, admitting that my way of giving feedback was failing my students freed me from trying to make it work or making excuses for why it wasn't working. It freed me from trying to force it to work or tweak it so that it would work or blame my kids when it didn't work. Once I admitted that my way was failing, I could stop trying to fix it and start from scratch.

And that's what I did. I sat in the cafeteria long after that faculty meeting finished and thought about why my current way of giving feedback didn't work. Slowly, I realized that it was because I was telling my students what to fix but not how to fix it. Thus, while my feedback pointed out mistakes, it didn't empower students to learn from them. What's more, it was much too complicated. My comments made it *harder* for students to focus on how to fix their errors, not easier. And my feedback was evaluative, rather than actionable. Students couldn't use it to understand their mistakes and correct them on their own.

> *While my feedback pointed out mistakes, it didn't empower students to learn from them. What's more, it was much too complicated.*

From there, I imagined a different kind of feedback. I called it color-coded grading and it immediately changed not only the way that I provided feedback, it changed the way that I taught. It's what made the difference between being a good teacher and becoming a master teacher.

I never would have gotten there if I hadn't admitted and learned from my failure, and yet, even now I find it hard to fail. But as hard as it is to fail, I know from experience that failing up is the only way to reach mastery. Failure is inevitable; learning from failure is a choice. We all will fail at some point. But if you can choose to admit failure and learn from it, then you're well on your way to becoming a master teacher.

BACK TO MY MISTAKE

I was sick to my stomach as I walked down to the main office after the class period was over. I filled out the paper work and went to teach my next class. That day my later classes, too, got a worksheet, and I stared out the window while they completed it in silence. At the end of the day, I packed my bags and walked down to see my department head and principal.

When I walked in, they sat at the table and looked at me sternly. "Robyn, take a seat," my principal gestured to a chair across from him. I sank into my seat and steeled myself for the yelling.

"What happened?" my department chair asked.

I shrugged. "I don't know. I had my back turned and was helping a student when I smelled the smoke and turned around to see that the lamp was on fire."

"How did it catch fire?" my principal asked.

"The students threw some paper into the top of it," I explained simply, sure that they were about to fire me.

The principal nodded. "What kind of lamp was it?" he asked.

What kind of lamp? I was confused. Why wasn't he firing me? I shrugged and described the lamp as best as I could remember.

"That's what I thought," the principal looked at my department chair meaningfully. "Those lamps are illegal to have in school," he explained to me and then turned back to my department chair. "Have Judy come see me," he requested and then stood up and walked out of the conference room.

I sat there confused. "You're not going to fire me?" I asked my boss.

She laughed long and hard. "Look, kiddo," she leaned back. "We all have our mistakes. Those lamps catch fire all the time, which is why they aren't allowed in school. It's really not your fault. Go home, get some rest. You had a tough day. It happens. You'll do better tomorrow."

I nodded and walked out to my car. My hands were shaking, so I just sat there in the driver's seat for a while thinking about my day. How could they be so nonchalant about the whole thing? I wondered. I still had that sick feeling in the pit of my stomach.

Tom, one of my colleagues, walked by my car. He saw me sitting there and stopped. I rolled down the window.

"I heard your kids set your classroom on fire today," he teased.

I hung my head.

"Oh. Too soon to joke about it?" he chuckled. "Come on, don't beat yourself up. It happens."

"It happens to bad teachers, Tom. It shouldn't have happened to me." My voice broke.

"Look, Robyn. We all make mistakes. You can't beat yourself up like this."

"Tom, my kids *set my classroom on fire.* How many times has that happened to you?"

"Twice."

I looked up at Tom, stunned. "Huh?"

"Twice." He repeated. "Once a kid tried to sneak a smoke in the classroom and lit his homework by accident. Another time some kids were playing with matches in their desk. Nothing caught on fire that time."

"You're just saying that to make me feel better." I did feel better.

"No," Tom shook his head. "I'm saying it to let you know that we all make mistakes. It happens. We're working with kids, and kids are unpredictable. They do stupid stuff. You're gonna mess up, believe me. But making mistakes doesn't make you a bad teacher. Not learning from them does."

He looked at me for a moment. "You're gonna beat yourself up about this for a while. We all do. But then you're gonna have to move on. Go home, take the night off, and give yourself a break. The kids will be waiting for you tomorrow."

I did beat myself up about the fire that night and for several nights after. I was embarrassed. But Tom was right. I had to move on. My kids had forgotten about it the next day.

―――

You, too, are going to make mistakes. Lots of them. Some of them will be embarrassing. There will be days when you feel like a total failure. There will be days when you feel like you'll never get good at teaching.

But mistakes are a very important part of becoming a master teacher. They can be some of your best lessons if you let them. You'll want to hide your mistakes, cover them up so that no one sees that you've messed up, but I urge you not to treat your mistakes that way. If you do, you'll miss out on some of the most powerful learning of your career. Instead, face your mistakes head on. Go ahead and let yourself feel the embarrassment that comes with them for a little while, but then choose to learn from your mistakes. It's one of the best ways to get better.

CHAPTER 8

YOU CAN GET BETTER
GROWING YOUR OWN
TEACHING STYLE

I used to feel really guilty about my first year of teaching. Although I'd done my best, when I looked back on all that I didn't know, I felt bad for my students. If I'd only known then what I know now, I could have been a much better teacher for them.

You'll hear this a lot from veteran teachers. They'll tell you how they wish they could go back and apologize to their first class, or they'll share war stories of their first year and then shake their heads and say, "Those poor kids." If you're not careful, you may start to feel guilty about your own first year, your own mistakes, and pity your own kids.

I have to tell you, I no longer feel guilty about my first year of teaching. I see it differently now. Instead of feeling sorry for my students for all the mistakes that I made, I am grateful to them for all that they taught me and proud of them for all that we were able to learn together. Why should I feel sorry for them? They got the best I had

> *Getting better is really about giving students your best every day.*

to offer them at the time every single day.

And that's really the point. Getting better is really about giving students your best every day. Yes, you will make mistakes. Yes, there is much that you still have to learn. But that doesn't mean that your students have to suffer through years of bumbling before you can provide them with an excellent education. Give your students the best that you have right now and know that you can get better. Here's how:

UNDERSTAND YOUR STANDARDS

I'm often surprised at how little emphasis is placed on teachers examining the standards by which they're evaluated. Even many veteran teachers I've met haven't studied their evaluation criteria and instruments. This is a huge mistake.

If you want to get better at your job, you need to understand what your district considers "better." I know that the evaluation process can be intimidating, but the best way to make it less so is to thoroughly understand the process for yourself.

I was working with a group of teachers recently who were really disgruntled. Their district had just changed their evaluation system to include a new set of standards. Additionally, about 40 percent of their evaluation would be based on their students' test scores. Not only were the teachers terrified that they would have to be accountable for their students' performance at a time when students were being asked to meet more rigorous learning standards and perform on newly revamped, more rigorous state tests, they were really intimidated by the new standards, which seemed impossible to actually meet.

By the time I began to work with them, they had worked themselves up into a real panic. They were afraid that they were going to lose their jobs. Although I was there to help them improve the level of rigor in their lessons, they spent much of the first hour complaining that rigor was too hard for their students.

I pushed back gently, "Why don't you believe that your students can actually meet the more rigorous standards?"

The room got quiet and a little tense. "Because our students are often two or three grade levels below when they get to us," one teacher explained.

"Not only that," another continued, "but these new tests are really hard. Our kids aren't used to being tested that way." Heads nodded in agreement.

"Have you looked at the new test?" I asked.

Eyes lowered. "Uh, no. Not exactly," they admitted. "But I hear it's really hard."

I turned to my laptop, closed my rigor presentation, and navigated to the state test web site. "Why don't we take a look at the test?" I suggested.

For the next twenty minutes, we tried a few sample items from the test. After we took each item, we stopped and tried to identify what kind of thinking was demanded by that item and what students would need to know and be able to do to successfully complete that test item. By the time we were finished, teachers had a much better sense of how students would be tested and what they would need to do in the classroom to help students pass that test.

Another time, it wasn't the state test that worried teachers; it was their new teacher evaluation standards themselves. I was working with a small group of fairly new teachers who had just gone through their first teacher evaluation. They had received feedback from their principals, and although some were simply relieved to have gotten through it, almost all of them felt that they hadn't scored as high as they would have liked.

Again, I was there to work with them on rigorous unit planning, but they were so distracted by their teacher evaluations that I decided to set my presentation aside and help them deal with their evaluation standards.

"How many of you studied the standards before your teacher evaluations?" I asked. Only a few raised their hands.

"How many of you would take a test without studying?" I asked.

They looked sheepish, but one person raised her hand and asked, "But how do you study for a teacher evaluation?" Other heads nodded in agreement.

"Good question," I smiled. "The first step is that you need to understand the evaluation criteria."

"But they went over that with us at one of our new teacher meetings," another teacher explained.

I nodded. "You need to do more than go over it. You need to unpack it a little so that you know exactly what you need to do to improve."

Over the next hour, we took a good look at their instrument. We started with the first domain and looked at the performance rubric. Then we started from the lowest rating and compared it to the next highest rating. Then we identified the *one thing* that they would need to do to move up from the lowest rating to the next rating in that category and so on. It was at times tedious work, but the discussions and debates that ensued as we looked for the "one thing" really helped clarify the evaluation instrument. Finally, I asked them to take out their own recently completed teacher observation reports. Then I asked them to use their unpacked rubric to set goals for their next observation. What were the one or two things they needed to do to get from where they were to the next level? By the end, not only did everyone understand how they were being evaluated, they also understood exactly what they needed to do to improve.

Most of us tend to ignore the very instruments by which we are going to be evaluated, but if you ignore them you're doing so at your own peril. If you'll be held accountable for students' test scores, you must completely understand the test they'll be taking. And if you're being held accountable to a set of teaching standards, then you really need to know the difference between one level and the next for each standard so that you know exactly how to improve. Doing so will not only take the anxiety out of the teacher evaluation process, it will actually help you improve your performance in the ways that count the most.

WORKING WITH ASSIGNED MENTORS

Finding a good mentor early in your career is one of the best ways that you can accelerate your own learning. A lot of districts will assign you a mentor, and navigating this relationship can take some finesse. The key thing to remember is that your mentor is not there to evaluate you. Instead, your mentor is there to help you become a better teacher. It seems obvious, but many new teachers forget this and simply try to do things the way that their mentor tells them to. That is not what mentoring is about.

> *Many new teachers try to do things the way that their mentor tells them to. That is not what mentoring is about.*

At your first meeting with your assigned mentor, spend some time sharing your goals for the year. What do you want to accomplish and what specific support do you think that you need? Don't be passive here. Even if you don't know exactly what kind of support you'll need, at least explain what supports you found most helpful in the past. Do you benefit from being observed and receiving feedback? What kind of feedback has been the most helpful? Would you like to get additional resources? Would it help to see demonstration lessons? Is there an educational author whose work you've found particularly helpful? Share all of this with your mentor as specifically as you can. The more that you establish, from the beginning, a focus on your goals and the supports you find most useful, the better equipped your mentor will be to help you achieve your goals.

Next, ask your mentor about his or her goals for supporting you. What does your mentor hope to help you learn? Listen carefully. You want to know early on whether the mentor's goals are more focused on helping you become your best self or whether their goals are more about accomplishing the benchmarks outlined by their job descriptions. Most likely, your mentor's goals will be some combination of the two, but you need to see where your mentor's focus will be. That will tell you early on exactly what kind of help you can count on from your mentor.

As you work with your mentor, be proactive. Don't just wait for your mentor to initiate contact or sit passively by and let your mentor run the relationship; you have a say in—and a responsibility for—how the relationship works as well. If you are not getting the support you want, ask your mentor for what you really need. Understand that not every mentor will meet every need that you have. You will likely need multiple mentors, both formal and informal, so don't look to your assigned mentor to meet all of your needs. Accept the help that your assigned mentor can give you and look for informal mentors in your colleagues to help with the areas where you still need support.

FINDING YOUR OWN MENTORS

Throughout your career you'll need to find informal mentors who can help you grow as a teacher. Here is what to look for if you are searching for a good mentor:

1. **Find someone who is willing to learn from you as much as they are willing to help you learn.** Ideally,

the mentorship relationship is a two-way street. You are not looking for Yoda here. You are looking for someone who gives as well as he or she gets. Someone who will listen to your ideas, ask your opinions, and accept your input. This way, your mentor will help you develop your own teaching style rather than push you to adopt theirs.

> *You don't want someone who has stopped learning. They can't help you learn.*

2. **Find someone who is still working on his or her own practice.** You don't want someone who has stopped learning. They can't help you learn. Instead, you want someone who is still tweaking their own teaching, refining their own approach. A person who is still learning can share the learning process with you. A person who feels there is nothing else to learn will have a harder time understanding that you are in a learning process yourself and will not provide you the support and space you need to engage in that learning process fully.

3. **Find someone who will tell you the truth, whether you want to hear it or not.** Some mentors will offer you pat solutions or prescribed "coaching talk." What you want is someone who will tell you the truth about your practice and will not sugar-coat it. We all

have blind spots in our practice. Until you deal with the truth, you can't make the substantive changes that will transform your teaching practice. Having a mentor who will point out your blind spots and help you see the truth of why something is or is not working will help you address the right parts of your teaching and improve them.

4. **Find someone who is a little different from you.** We tend to gravitate toward people who share our same perspective, but there is huge benefit from hearing a different opinion. It forces us to examine what we believe, see things from a different vantage point, and consider ideas that might not have occurred to us otherwise. You won't always agree, but your practice will benefit from hearing a different point of view.

5. **Find someone who has actually achieved the results you want to achieve.** There is no point in receiving advice from someone who hasn't actually put their own advice into practice. If you struggle with classroom management, find someone who has figured it out for themselves. If you need help with planning, look for someone who knows how to plan. Don't listen to pat advice. Look for someone who has already walked the journey you're just beginning and has actually been successful in the key areas where you struggle.

MAKE THE MOST OF
EVERY PROFESSIONAL
DEVELOPMENT OPPORTUNITY

I've sat through my share of really bad PD. In fact, I got really good at being able to tell whether a workshop was going to be useful within the first five minutes, and if I determined that I wasn't going to get anything out of it, I'd quickly tune out. I even carried a "workshop survival kit" with things I could do to surreptitiously occupy myself while pretending to participate. I thought I was being polite and more than a little clever, but really, I was wasting valuable opportunities to learn.

A few years into my teaching career, I started taking a different approach to PD. I decided that no matter how bad it was, I would try to get something from it. At the very least, I wanted to take the time away from my classroom to work on my own teaching. So rather than occupy myself on my phone or secretly grade papers, I would bring materials that were related to the workshop and try to apply what I was learning to my classroom. Sometimes, I will admit, it was a struggle to find something valuable in a workshop or district-enforced PD. But when I came to each session with the attitude that there was always something I could learn, I would find little hidden gems that ignited my own thinking and helped me refine my practice.

I remember one workshop that really bored me. We were in the midst of a curriculum rollout and were forced to sit through an entire day of people reading the new curriculum binders to us, punctuated with a few "team-building" activities that usually involved chart paper, markers, and a group hug at the end. I rolled my eyes through much of the morning, and I spent the entire lunch hour cynically rehashing all the ways that the workshop that morning had violated every single principle of "good teaching" with my equally annoyed colleagues.

By the end of lunch, I had worked myself up so much that I had a horrible attitude going into the afternoon session. As soon as the first PowerPoint slide went up, I rolled my eyes and slouched in my chair and began to stew. My mind was entirely closed. About ten minutes into the presentation, I noticed that a woman seated at my table was paying rapt attention and furiously scribbling down notes. *What on earth is she writing?* I wondered, and leaned over to peek at her paper. She was writing what looked like lesson plans. During the next "think, pair, share" activity, I partnered with her and asked her what she was doing. She showed me how she had adapted what we had been shown that morning to tweak her lesson planning process. As a result, she had already mapped out much of her next unit.

"You got *that* from the nonsense we were doing this morning?" I asked incredulously.

She nodded. "Something the presenter said sparked an idea in my head. Then I started to scribble a few ideas down and soon, I figured out how I might make it work for my lesson plans. I'll play with it a little more this afternoon and see if it will really work. If so, I'll use it. If not," she shrugged. "At least I got to play around with a new idea today. Something's bound to come of it."

We were both at the same workshop, but while I was having a miserable time, she was getting better. It was a profound lesson for me, and I have used that approach ever since. No matter how bad the workshop, I'm determined to learn something.

The first thing I do is that I go to workshops with a selfish attitude. That doesn't mean that I hog all the good markers and talk over the presenter. It means that for everything the presenter says, I immediately think of how it might apply to my own teaching situation. Everything. Even if it seems unrelated, I keep thinking about it

I go to workshops with a selfish attitude. For everything the presenter says, I immediately think of how it might apply to my own teaching situation.

until I find a connection. This expands my thinking and makes even those things that seem irrelevant useful.

Second, if something isn't clear, I ask questions until I understand. Occasionally a presenter will skip over my questions or relegate them to the "parking lot," but that's okay. I ask the questions anyway. Sometimes I get the answers, but even if I don't get the answer from the presenter, I often get answers from the other participants. And if I walk away from the workshop without a good answer, I go home and research it on my own. Asking questions is one method that helps me stay engaged.

Finally, I learned from my friend and colleague Max Thompson the idea of "adapt, don't adopt." Every new idea I encounter, I immediately look to see if I can adapt it to my own purposes. I don't try to adopt an idea wholesale. I look to see how I can tweak it so that it fits me. This has allowed me to take even a seemingly bad idea and turn it into something useful for my own practice. And it opens my mind to the possibilities I might not have noticed otherwise.

PICK YOUR BATTLES

If you're like me, you went into teaching intending to change the world. You want to make a difference. You want to transform lives. And you will. Just not the way you think.

A lot of first-year teachers I know are outraged at the way the system works. They go into their classrooms with ideals and are appalled at all the ways in which school systems are imperfect or downright broken. And they want to correct it all right away. Or they're shocked at the needs that their students bring with them to school each day and want to overcome all of the inequities of poverty and race and gender right now.

Believe me, I get it. It feels almost immoral not to do *something*. But trying to fix every wrong that you see is a sure way to frustration and burnout. You can't fall into this trap. You've got to pick your battles. Otherwise you'll become disillusioned quickly.

Don't get me wrong here. I'm not saying that we just live with the things that are wrong or accept injustice. Oh, no—that isn't what I am saying at all. It is our moral imperative to fight against these things. Our students need us to advocate on their behalf. Many school systems are broken. Inequity lurks in far too many places. There are things in every school that are inefficient or unfair, and these things need fixing. But if you rush in and try to fix it all at once, you will burn out. Take time to understand what it is that you're fighting. Determine the root cause rather than try to fight the symptoms so that you can actually make a difference.

A LOT OF WHAT YOU LEARNED IN SCHOOL WILL NEVER WORK FOR YOU

It isn't because what they taught you in school was wrong technically. It's just that everything you learned may not work in your particular situation or with your individual teaching style.

I remember going to a workshop at which the dynamic presenter showed us a great strategy to teach close reading of text. It was rather involved, but I took careful notes and couldn't wait to try it with my class. The next week, I unveiled my new strategy to my students, and they gamely played along. They really wanted it to work because *I* wanted it to work. So we all went through the motions, but to no avail. The strategy was a solid one; it just wasn't the right fit for my students' needs or my own teaching style. I thought at first that I must be doing it wrong because it had been so successful for the teacher who had presented it. It had literally transformed her classroom! But it didn't transform my class. I persisted, tweaked it, and invested way more time and energy than it was worth trying to make it work. And it did work…sort of. But something wasn't right. I knew it. My kids knew it.

It took a long time for me to realize that the problem wasn't the strategy. It was a good strategy for a certain kind of kid in a certain kind of classroom. It just wasn't the right strategy for *us*. Had I understood my own teaching and the purpose of the strategy better, I would have been able to tell it wasn't a right fit. But I grabbed onto something I thought would work without really understanding how it might—or in this case might not—work for me.

I see it happen all the time: teachers I observe using strategies they learned in school or in workshops that are not a good fit for their classrooms. I even see teachers in my workshops eagerly writing down a strategy and vowing to use it with their students *tomorrow* without taking the time to examine why the strategy works and determining whether it will work for them.

Not everything you learn in school or at a workshop will actually work for you. It may be that a strategy is a great one, but not the appropriate one for you, your students, or your teaching style. Other times the strategy may look good and yet have no substance or contribute nothing to your students' progress. There's a saying in dominos that "all money ain't good money." It means that not every point you earn will actually help you win. Sometimes in players' eagerness to earn points, they end up missing other, more valuable points or give more points away than they earn. The same is true in teaching. Not all money is good money. Sometimes a strategy may make perfect sense on paper, may have research and theory behind it, may even have worked for thousands of teachers before you, and still not be the right fit for your students. Be strategic. Choose only those strategies that fit your teaching style, your students' needs, and your instructional goals for the year. Ask yourself the following questions:

- Is this a good fit for the way that I teach or the way that I have my classroom arranged?
- Who has used this strategy successfully, and does my teaching style or student population match his or hers?
- How will my students respond?
- Does this directly match their learning needs/styles?
- How does this strategy help me reach my instructional goals?
- Is there a quicker, easier, more direct way to accomplish what I am trying to accomplish with students?
- Will the investment in this strategy be worth what I think the payoff will be?
- How much time will this strategy take, and can I afford to spend that kind of time?

Use these questions to vet any strategy you are considering. Then make wise choices about which strategies you'll use and which you will save for another time. Remember, it may be a great strategy, just not a great match for you.

※

It can be hard being the new kid on the block. You look around you and everyone else seems to have it all together. Sometimes you can feel like you're bumbling your way through the year. Sometimes you'll be so overwhelmed by all that you don't know that you lose sight of what you *do* know. Be gentle with yourself. You're still learning. And if you want to get really good at your job, you'll never stop learning.

So stop feeling guilty about all that you don't know yet and stop feeling sorry for your students. You're working hard. You're learning. You're growing. And in the process, you're giving your students the best you've got.

CHAPTER 9

YOU CAN SHINE

DISTINGUISHING YOURSELF AS AN EDUCATOR

I was giving a speech at a conference recently, and during the break, a young lady approached me. After introducing herself and complimenting me on my speech, she said, "May I ask you a question?"

"Sure," I smiled.

"How do I do what you do?"

"What I do?" I asked, not quite sure what she meant.

"Be a consultant," she explained. "I want to consult and give speeches and write books like you do."

"Okay," I said cautiously. "May I ask you a personal question?"

"Sure," she nodded.

"Um," I wasn't sure how to begin. She looked so young. "How long have you been teaching?"

Her brow wrinkled, and she crossed her arms. "I'm in my second year. But I'm twenty-four, and I am almost finished with my master's degree."

"I see," I replied, trying to figure out what to say next.

"Look, I know what you're about to say," she began. "You're going to tell me that I'm too young and that I need to 'pay my dues' and 'put in my time.'" She used air quotes. "But I'm smart, okay? I want to do more than just teach my whole life. Life is really short, and I have goals."

I get this a lot. Young teachers who have aspirations beyond the classroom approach me all the time and ask me how they, too, can become consultants or start their own businesses. Their question always makes me a little sad. I miss the classroom every day, and it seems that many of them cannot wait to escape it.

And yet, I understand their ambition. I get their impatience with the advice that they have to "pay their dues." Many of you are smart and talented and have so much to offer the world. Why sit back and wait your turn?

You want to make an impact outside of your classroom. You have goals and ambitions for something more than what you're doing right now. Perhaps you're frustrated with the often condescending advice to "put in your time" or "wait your turn." You want to shine right now.

Here's how you can.

BECOME YOUR BEST

I gave a training recently to a group of new or nearly new teachers about how to implement rigorous instruction.

That night, I got this e-mail from an aspiring teacher: "I am a senior in Elementary Education. To be honest, I went [to your workshop] last week so that I could have something else that would 'look good' on my resume. As a future teaching position applicant, I'm always trying to find things that will make me 'look good.' I am now inspired and motivated to not only look good, but to be good…Do you have any tips or suggestions for a future applicant when it comes to the teaching field? I have been told that the number of applicants per position is 267 in [my desired school system]. I want to do what I can to stand out to principals and have a teaching job next fall."

> *The more that you focus on looking good, the more shallow your practice will be.*

As I wrote her back, I applauded this teacher for her initiative and for her epiphany. It is more about being good than looking good, and the irony is that the better you are, the better you look. It's a hard transition from looking for a job and polishing your resume to being in a job and doing your best, but it is an important one. The more that you focus on looking good, the more shallow your practice will be. The more that you focus on being good, the more solid your practice will be. And believe me, people will take notice. That's the thing about shining. You shine best when you are at your best. Be your best. Don't worry about how you look. If you *are* good, you'll look good.

LEARN FROM EVERYONE

When I first started teaching, I suffered from a bit of hubris. I was fresh out of graduate school, full of the latest ideas in education, and believed (rather smugly) that I was very talented. I entered a department where all of my colleagues were between ten and forty years older than I, and many of them seemed to my young eyes to be past their prime. I would never have admitted it, but I honestly thought that although my colleagues may have had more experience than I, their experience was so outdated, so antiquated, that it was of little use to me. What made it worse is that some of the older teachers in my department were a bit eccentric, and I didn't want to be anything like them.

One teacher in my department was universally reviled by her colleagues. Julie was abrasive, pushy, and sometimes downright rude to her colleagues and students. She rarely remembered her students' names, yelled at them, and was unrelenting in her demands for their work. At least that's what I had been told.

Julie and I taught the same course and often exchanged students at the semester break because of scheduling changes. Having heard the stories about Julie, I, quite smugly, thought that I was the better teacher. After all, I was warm, I was encouraging, and I knew all of my students' names by the second week of the semester. Although Julie had offered to share resources with me, I politely refused, preferring to use my own materials. When we had to meet as a team, I pretended to listen to her ideas but dismissed them as soon as the meeting was done. Otherwise, I stayed away from her as much as possible, afraid that she might corrupt the purity of my pedagogy by her mere proximity.

One day I took my students into the computer lab after Julie's students had just finished using it and found one of my former students' papers left on the printer. I was curious to see how his writing had progressed since he had left my class for hers, so I casually read over his paper. I was shocked by how much he'd improved. Many of the things that he had struggled with in my classroom seemed corrected in hers. It was a sobering blow. How, I wondered, had she been able to help him when I had failed to?

That afternoon, I returned his paper to Julie and shyly asked her how she had managed to help him improve his writing so much. Julie beamed and then spent the next thirty minutes explaining to me how she taught students to structure their papers and the scaffolds she provided. Though I didn't agree with everything she did, I learned a lot from that session. After that, I began to meet with Julie on a regular basis and soak up as much as possible from her. Some things I knew wouldn't work for me, but a lot of her methods were quite sound, and as I incorporated them into my own practice, I saw immediate improvement in my students. Julie remained all that she was, but I no longer found her annoying. Instead, she and I forged a wonderful collegial relationship that lasted until she retired. Julie taught me a lot.

As my father always reminds me, even a broken clock is right twice a day. Remember that when you work with your colleagues. You can learn something valuable from every one of them. Don't dismiss anyone. Soak up all that you can from everyone you meet. In fact, look for the valuable learning experiences every one of your colleagues can bring to you—even if you have to dig for it. Doing so can significantly accelerate your learning curve and round out your teaching.

FIND YOUR PASSION

Although leadership positions can look glamorous from the vantage point of a chaotic classroom, administration can be really grueling work. And the rewards are a lot less tangible outside the classroom than in the classroom. If you're going to commit your life and career to climbing the ladder, you need to make sure that you do so in a way that still feeds and honors your passion.

Success for success's sake is an empty existence. I remember one colleague who, after a few years of teaching, became an instructional coach. We got together to celebrate, and she spoke excitedly of how she hoped to really shine in her new position. A year later, she called me to lament how disappointed she was. She thought that as an instructional coach, she would have more power. She thought that the position would mean that her colleagues would listen to her and implement her suggestions. She learned very quickly that as an instructional coach, you have very little power. In fact, you may have even less power than you did in the classroom.

Not long after, she decided that she wanted to become an assistant principal, and within a year, she found an AP position. When I called to congratulate her, she beamed, "Now I'll be able to get some things done!" I warned her that as an AP, she'd have even less control over her own time, but she laughed off the warnings. Instead, she talked excitedly about how she would finally get an office of her own and be a twelve-month employee. And the raise!

A year later she called me to again express her disappointment. It wasn't what she thought it would be. The teachers hated her. They didn't listen. She was working long hours and never saw her children. The work was tedious and unrewarding. She talked about how she was going to try to become a principal because at least then, she would be in charge. Or, maybe she would try for a central office job and get out of the school completely.

Pursuing a promotion for the sake of a promotion doesn't necessarily lead to happiness. Even if you'd be making more money and your resume would look fantastic, the next job isn't guaranteed to fulfill you, especially when you're seeking an "ascent" more than seeking your passion. Some people are always looking for the next promotion, climbing their way to the top regardless of whether each new job aligns with what they really want to do with their lives. Others have found their passion, and each promotion they get is a direct result of pursuing that passion. Guess which group is happier?

UNDERSTAND YOUR SCHOOL SYSTEM

When you first start teaching, it's easy to be so consumed with what is going on in your classroom that you miss what is going on outside your classroom. In my early years of teaching, it was hard enough for me to keep track of my students, my curriculum, and the dynamics of my school building. I had little time to pay attention to the politics of my district.

I taught in a very large school district with a huge central office. We had a weekly newsletter that was distributed throughout the district, but I rarely read it. We also had a district website, but I used it mostly to handle things like scheduling substitutes and managing my payroll paperwork. I thought that all I had to do was focus on what was happening in my school.

The summer after my first year, I received a call from someone in central office (sadly, I had no idea who she was or even her position). She asked me to be one of three first-year teachers to give a "welcome back to school" speech to the incoming new teachers for the coming school year. At the time, I didn't understand what a big deal that was. I figured it would be me in a room with a hundred or so new teachers and I could just tell them about a few of my first year experiences, give them a few pieces of advice that had helped me through my first year, and wish them luck. I agreed without giving it much thought and went to visit my family, who lived in another state at the time. I wrote out a quick talk on the plane and edited it when I got home.

My first clue that this was going to be a big deal was when someone from central office (again, I had no idea who) called me at home and asked me to fax in a copy of my speech. Then yet another person called me to walk me through the protocol for the day and remind me of the dress code. I realized then that the district took this speech pretty seriously, so I tinkered with my talk, made it more of a speech, and rehearsed it a few times in front of the mirror.

The day arrived, and I drove to one of the high schools in the district in a neighborhood I had never visited before. There were literally hundreds of cars parked in the lot. I finally found a space, parked, and nervously walked into the school. There was a band playing, hundreds of people milling around drinking coffee, signs everywhere welcoming the new teachers, and a table out front giving out bags and name badges. I approached the table, announced who I was, and was handed a packet with the schedule and a name badge. I took my packet gingerly and walked into the auditorium.

When my eyes adjusted to the dim lights in the auditorium, I was immediately stunned. There were several thousand people already seated. Several members of the press were setting up cameras to film. People with clipboards were scurrying to and fro getting ready. I froze. This would be my audience?

I took a deep breath and walked down to the front. I stood there for a minute, unsure of what to do or where to sit. I noticed two gentlemen in suits standing near the stage and thought that they might be able to help, so I approached them.

"Excuse me," I politely interrupted their conversation. They turned and faced me, smiling. "I'm sorry to interrupt, but I was wondering if either of you knew who was in charge here."

The gentlemen chuckled. The taller one pointed to the other and said, "He's in charge."

The other gentleman shook his head, "Oh, no. I work for him," he said pointing to the first man. They both broke out into laughter.

I looked confused. I had obviously missed the joke. The first gentleman saw my confusion and smiled. "How can we help you?" he asked.

"Well, I'm supposed to give a speech today on the program but I'm not sure where I'm supposed to sit," I pointed to my name on the program.

They looked at my name listed on the program and noticed my school. "Ah, you work at that high school?" the second gentleman asked.

"Yes," I smiled.

"How do you like it?" he asked.

"Well, I've only been working there for six months, but so far, I love it."

"Six months?" He looked at the first gentleman in mock horror. "You mean to tell me that we have this young woman speaking to the new teachers with only six months' experience?" They both began to laugh.

"I don't know," the first gentleman shook his head.

I caught the joke. "Don't worry, gentlemen. I'm just that good," I bragged playfully.

We stood there joking for a few more minutes until the master of ceremonies approached the podium and asked everyone to take their seats. I looked up in a panic because I still didn't know where I was supposed to sit. The first gentleman saw my panic and motioned for me to follow him. "Here, you can come sit with us," he offered.

I sat on the end of the first row with the two gentlemen and nervously looked at my speech. The master of ceremonies welcomed everyone to the event and announced that this year, the district had hired 2,200 new teachers, most of whom were there that day. 2,200? Oh, boy.

I tuned out a lot of the preliminary talks and studied my speech. Soon, someone (of course, I had no idea who she was) introduced the superintendent of schools. I looked up to the stage, curious to see who he was, and to my utter horror, the second gentleman from my earlier conversation got up, winked at me, and walked to the stage.

I was mortified. I thought back to how I had cavalierly joked with him not five minutes before, and my face burned with embarrassment. I was humiliated that I had had no idea who he was and he knew it. I felt like a complete idiot.

I got through my speech fine and survived the day, but I learned an important lesson that I've never forgotten. If I'm going to be part of a system, I need to know the players and how the system works. I should have done my research ahead of time. If I had, I would have known that my system typically hired several thousand new teachers each year and could have been prepared for the crowd. If I had done my research, I would have known who the people were who invited me to speak. If I had done my research, I would have known the superintendent and his deputy when I met them.

Do your research. Understand how your school system works. Take time to look at the organizational chart for central office so that you can see who makes the decisions that directly affect you. Look at the superintendent's strategic plan. Understand who is on your school board and how the board works. Read the district's newsletter. Set up a Google alert to stay abreast of news about your school district. You don't have to get caught up in the politics, but it's important to understand how they work, because they do affect you in several ways:

For one, the policies that govern your work come out of the politics of your district. Decisions on everything from salary increases to new curricular requirements are made at the district level, so it's good to keep up. Second, if you want to move in your district beyond the classroom someday, it's important to know what other jobs are available and what they entail. Even if you want to stay in the classroom, it's important to know what other opportunities—summer employment or extra duties you can take on, for example—exist within the district. Many summers, I've done work for the district to pick up extra money. I have also worked on extra paid projects during the school year to help make ends meet as well as to get exposure to other aspects of the profession. Many of those jobs came from simply knowing that they were available because I kept track of what was going on at the district level. Later, I was afforded other opportunities because I knew the right person in central office.

Learn how your district works. Not only can it save you

> *Learn how your district works. It can help you shine by exposing you to opportunities you may have missed otherwise.*

extreme embarrassment, it can help you shine by exposing you to opportunities you may have missed otherwise.

MAKE PROFESSIONAL CONNECTIONS OUTSIDE YOUR SCHOOL

One of the most important things you can do to foster your own growth and development is to get exposure beyond your district. Learning from colleagues in other districts, states, or countries can significantly expand your teaching skills, give you exposure to new ideas, and keep you from becoming myopic. A great way to make outside professional contacts is to get involved in professional organizations locally and nationally. Attend professional conferences and broaden your knowledge and expertise by learning from others. While you're there, watch carefully how the best presenters present, and then submit a conference proposal or two of your own.

This is how I got my start as a consultant. I began my speaking career by submitting a proposal to present at a district-wide professional development conference. After that presentation, I was invited to present at a state-wide conference, and from there, I was encouraged to submit that same proposal for a national conference. My proposal was accepted, and I began presenting at other national conferences, where I met and learned from colleagues across the globe. Not only did these experiences hone my skills, make me a better teacher, and ultimately prepare me to be a consultant, they put me in touch with national experts who served as mentors and coaches to me throughout my career.

FOCUS ON YOUR STUDENTS

Oftentimes, in our attempts to get really good and be noticed, we forget that the best barometer of our expertise is the impact that we make on our students. Don't lose sight of that. If you focus on your students, on giving them the very best you can, you will shine. People will take notice.

This really hit home for me one year after I had been teaching for about four years. I had met a reporter from the *Washington Post* who was interested in seeing how I was helping minority and low–socioeconomic status students succeed in advanced placement (AP) courses. He asked if he could come by my classroom and watch me teach and then possibly include me in an article he was working on about opening access to AP courses.

I was thrilled! This was a pretty famous reporter, and to have him include me in an article for his weekly column was incredibly exciting. I immediately started prepping my students. I prepared a model lesson and drilled my students ahead of time so that I was sure to look impressive when he arrived.

That day, he sat in the back of my classroom while I worked my way through my carefully scripted lesson. The only problem was that although my students were trying their best to make me look good, they got stuck on one item in, of all things, my warm-up. They just couldn't figure out a sentence they were working on.

At first, I tried to gamely talk them through the sentence, and they just as gamely tried to play along. But it was soon obvious that they just weren't getting it. I was mortified. I had two choices at that moment. I could have just put that warm-up item aside and moved on to the more interesting and impressive parts of my lesson, or I could forget that there was a reporter in the room and help my students.

After turning over the options in my head, I knew what I had to do: I chose my students. I took a deep breath, picked up a dry erase marker, and wrote the sentence they were struggling to understand on the board. I had been secretly teaching my students how to diagram sentences, both to parse difficult sentences and to improve their own sentence structure. At the time, sentence diagramming was seriously out of style. In fact, many experts considered it akin to torture and of little to no educational value. But because it seemed to work for my students, I would sneak in a lesson every now and again. I was terrified that anyone would find out that I was diagramming sentences, because the strategy was considered so archaic, but it really helped my students grapple with more difficult texts.

I shot one last embarrassed look at the famous reporter and then asked my students to diagram the sentence they were struggling to understand. About halfway through the diagram, the students suddenly understood it and were able to answer the question on the warm-up. I was thrilled for my students, but I taught the rest of the lesson with a gnawing feeling in the pit of my stomach. There just went my fifteen minutes of fame.

After the class period, I gingerly approached the reporter and asked him whether he had gotten what he hoped to get. He seemed distracted. I started to explain my lesson, but he interrupted me and said, "How long have you been teaching sentence diagramming?"

I hung my head and mumbled something about how I only used it every once in a while to help my students grapple with difficult texts. "I know it's a little unconventional," I laughed nervously. "But it seems to really help my students."

"That's interesting," he murmured as he put on his coat. "Thanks for letting me drop by." And with that, he—and my chance at fame—walked out of my classroom.

On my drive home, I started beating myself up for diagramming sentences in front of the reporter. I should have just moved on. I still believed in sentence diagramming as a tool, but I shouldn't have shown him. Now he thinks I'm a bad teacher, I brooded.

Imagine my surprise when, a few days later, he sent me an e-mail asking me a few more questions about how I used sentence diagramming. I answered his questions, defending my use of the strategy to help my students think through complex texts. A few days after that, he wrote me again and said that he was featuring my unconventional approach in an article in the *Washington Post*. He sent a photographer to my classroom to take pictures of me, and that Sunday, my picture and the article were on the front page of the metro section!

If I had chosen to look good rather than do what I knew was best for my students, I would have never had that opportunity to shine. At best, I could expect a mention somewhere in the body of his weekly column. But, by choosing to do what I thought was best for my kids no matter how it might have made me look, I ended up receiving more recognition than I'd originally hoped.

You'll always shine best when you focus on your students instead of yourself. Invest in them, not your career. Help them shine, and you'll shine too.

~~~

I know that you have goals and dreams about what you want to do with your life. You have ambition. You want to be the best, to rise through the ranks, and to be recognized for your accomplishments. There's nothing wrong with that. But I urge you to enjoy the ride. I have friends who are principals at thirty-five, superintendents at forty, and look around wondering what they'll do with the rest of their lives. I've also met many teachers young and old who are so focused on getting ahead that they fail to enjoy the ride. It's sad, really. These are some of the best days of your career. It's the time when you're learning what it means to be a great teacher and developing your own philosophy of education, your own teaching style, and your own teaching life. These moments may not feel like it right now, but they are precious. Don't miss them.

It's perfectly okay to have ambition, to want to get ahead. You can shine, but the glow that lasts cannot be sustained simply by landing the next job, the great promotion, or a more glamorous life. The shine comes from within. Find your passion and map your career based on what feeds you. That's the way to truly shine and make that shine last.

CHAPTER 10

YOU CAN LEAD
BECOMING A MASTER TEACHER

Y ou won't be a master teacher on your first day, or your first week, or even your first year. You will have moments that are masterful, but true mastery is consistent and seamless. It takes time to get there.

Don't let that discourage you.

You were probably a good student yourself and are used to "getting" things right away. You got good grades in your classes and were excited about finally getting to implement everything you learned in your own classroom. You spent weeks preparing, anticipating your students and the cool things you would help them learn.

But on your first day, or your first week, or your first month, things deviated from your plans. You hit a snag or encountered a challenge they didn't teach you about in school. You made a mistake or two, or maybe ten. You felt awkward and unprepared, maybe even a little overwhelmed. Back in your teacher prep program, you had no idea how much you didn't know.

It may feel like you'll never be a master teacher, never walk into a classroom and instantly sense exactly what you have to do to help students learn. It may feel like you will never get your classroom completely organized and all your students learning at the exact same time. But if you put in the work, it will happen. It just may not happen on your schedule.

Like I said, mastery takes time. Don't worry; I'm not going to go into a "you've gotta pay your dues" speech here. I'm simply sharing a truth that took me a while to learn. You see, I thought I was pretty good when I first started teaching. Sure, I had my challenges, but my first year wasn't entirely awful. In fact, there were even a few moments of brilliance if I say so myself.

But my second year of teaching presented new challenges. All the classroom management issues that typically characterize the first year happened to me during my second year of teaching. I don't really know why, either. I think it had a lot to do with the fact that I came in during the middle of the school year, when much of the classroom culture was

> *My first year wasn't half bad. But my second year of teaching presented new challenges.*

already established. My second year, I had to establish the culture myself, and I struggled.

What made it worse was that I thought that I was through all the first-year struggles. I thought that I had things down pat and was on my way to mastery. To struggle at that point made me

Everyone's path to mastery looks a little different.

question myself and, for a while, lose confidence in my ability to master teaching.

What I learned—and what you will learn, too—is that everyone's path to mastery looks a little different. Some of you will struggle mightily your first few months, start to figure things out around January or February, and emerge from your first year triumphant. Others of you will fly through your first year but hit roadblocks during your second or third year and want to leave the profession altogether. Others of you will make steady, incremental growth toward mastery. And still others of you will struggle your first few years and try several different approaches until you find one that works for you.

Each of us has our own path and our own timing. And those who don't reach mastery fail not because they didn't choose the right path, but because they gave up too soon.

Mastery, real mastery, takes time. You can't give up or get frustrated because you aren't getting better on your schedule or in the way that you imagined. Keep investing, keep trusting, and keep working. It will happen.

FIND YOUR *WHY*

The teachers who stay in teaching, those who become really great teachers, are those who find and live their *why*. If you lose sight of why you want to teach, the challenges of teaching will overwhelm you. Your why will give you focus, it will give you energy on the days when you are discouraged, it will give you the commitment to stick with a kid you'd rather give up on or to persist with doing the right thing even when everything seems to conspire against it. Your why will feed your passion. Your why will ignite your creativity. Your why will show you how to become a master teacher and let you know when you've made it there.

Perhaps you already know your why. Maybe you want to make a difference, or you want to help students love math, or you want to show students that they have options and possibilities. Wonderful! Do whatever you can to hold onto that why and find a way to feed it each day. Don't let a day go by without making a small difference, or helping one student come a little closer to loving math, or showing at least one student his possibilities, no matter how small.

Or maybe you're not yet sure of your why. You know that you enjoy teaching and working with students and you

may even feel that the
work you're doing is
important and mean-
ingful, but you're not
sure why it's important
and meaningful *to you*.

> *A borrowed why may be inspiring for a while, but it won't feed you and sustain you when things get tough.*

You're working with a why you've borrowed from a book
or from your school's mission statement or from the excitement generated by the organization that recruited you
to teaching. But I urge you to find your own why. A borrowed why may be inspiring for a while, but it won't feed
you and sustain you when things get tough. You have to
have your own very personal reasons for why you are
teaching. Otherwise, you're vulnerable to cynicism—or
worse, disillusionment—every time you face frustration.

Some of you may have lost your why. The demands of
your job, the pressures you're under, and the disillusionment you may feel at the difference between your ideals
and your reality may have caused you to abandon your why
or feel that you just can't accomplish it in your current situation. It can happen to any of us.

But you must find it again. You must. Otherwise
you do yourself and your students a disservice. Your
why will show you the way through disillusionment, and
it will shore you up against developing cynicism. Your
why will help you infuse meaning into your work even
when what you are currently being asked to do seems

meaningless. Your why will help you maintain your passion in even the worst of circumstances.

And that really is the point. Some teachers I work with have lost their why and are "phoning it in" by the time they come to me. These teachers are just getting through the day—overworked, overwhelmed, and sometimes over-wrought. They want solutions but have given up hope that things can actually get better. I've learned over the years that these feelings are a direct result of losing sight of your why. So the work I do with them is really around helping them reconnect with and find ways to feed their own why. The difference is almost always immediate and dramatic. We haven't changed their situation; the demands and pres-sures still exist. But somehow, when you reconnect with your why, all those things that seemed impossible suddenly seem doable.

That's the power of finding and protecting your why.

ACCEPT THE MESSINESS

Becoming a master teacher is the hardest, most demand-ing, and ultimately most rewarding thing any of us will ever do. But it's messy. There isn't a linear path to mastery. You'll finally get good at one part of your practice only to realize that another part needs work. Or you'll work hard at fixing one part of your practice and in the process have to readjust two other aspects. And sometimes, it isn't pretty.

I really struggled with the idea that becoming a master teacher was a messy process. It didn't seem as if it should be. After

> *The master teachers I knew made it all look so easy and effortless. I felt like a bumbling amateur by comparison.*

all, the master teachers I knew made it all look so easy and effortless. I felt like a bumbling amateur by comparison.

At first, I tried to hide my faults and pretend that I had it all together. I did a lot of the things I was already good at and avoided the things that were hard for me. That meant that I focused more on teaching writing, which I was good at, and less on helping my students develop better reading skills—an area where I had very little comfort or expertise. As a result, my teaching became rigid and uneven, and my students suffered for it. They became competent writers, yes, but they really struggled with reading and understanding literature.

My students' test scores ratted me out. They were so uneven that I couldn't hide my weaknesses any longer. I had to get better at teaching reading. At first I was resistant. It was uncomfortable admitting that there was a part of teaching in which I struggled. What was worse, I didn't know how to fix it.

I started researching reading strategies, but, because there are so many strategies and methods out there, I wasn't sure which one would work. I was afraid to try anything for fear that if I didn't pick the right one, I'd make things worse for my students. I asked around for help from my colleagues, but each of them did something different. It seemed as if each had picked something that worked for them, but I wasn't sure if any of it would work for me. The few strategies I did try felt awkward and clumsy. My students were starting to get impatient with my lack of direction and were treating many of my efforts to improve their reading as busy work.

I floundered for almost an entire grading period before I stumbled on something that worked for me. I sat in on a workshop where we were given a packet of strategies on teaching language arts. One of the strategies was a writing strategy, and yet I could see its potential for teaching close reading of passages. I played with it for a week or two and then tried it with my students. They responded well, and after trying it for a few days, I felt comfortable enough that I began to develop confidence and some proficiency with the technique. I had finally found a strategy that fit, and the difference for my students was almost immediate.

In fact, it was so successful that after a few weeks, it was hard to remember that it had taken months—and a lot of failed attempts—to find that strategy. If I had given up at any point in the process, if I had let the messiness of it all deter me, I never would have persisted until I found something that worked.

To this day I hate the messiness of getting better. I want to see a teaching problem, spend ten minutes thinking it through in my magical thinking cave, and emerge with *the answer* and benevolently share it with the waiting world. But even now, I find myself wrestling and sometimes floundering with every new challenge. I've been teaching and coaching teachers for a long time, and I can tell you, the messiness

> *Take away the messiness, take away the struggle, and you take away the learning.*

never goes away. In fact, I've come to accept it as a necessary part of the process of becoming and remaining a master teacher. Take away the messiness, take away the struggle, and you take away the learning.

So don't try to sanitize the process. Accept the messiness that comes with learning. It's uncomfortable, it's disconcerting, it's even frustrating, but the process of grappling with the mess and cleaning it up is where you'll find your best insights and make your greatest growth in your journey toward master teaching.

~~~

Lately, more and more teachers are coming up to me during workshops or after speeches and confiding that they're thinking about leaving the profession. They tell me how hard it is to actually teach with all the pressures of testing and the indignities they must face inside and outside the classroom. They talk about a lack of administrative support or how disrespectful the students and parents are. Many of them came into this profession with a passion for teaching or a real desire to make a difference, and somewhere along the way, the conditions of teaching sucked away all that passion. They lost hope.

It breaks my heart every time. They're leaving the best of professions. There is no other profession where you get to touch lives as profoundly as teaching. You get to help students learn, discover the world, and become their best selves.

Yes, the reality is that you will face unprecedented testing pressures. Yes, you will come up against unreasonable parents or disrespectful students. Yes, you will work long hours for a salary that doesn't fully compensate you for all that you do. Yes, you will face outside criticism from others who don't comprehend or value what you do, who shrug and say "anyone can teach."

The reality is also that you will help a child discover their own potential and their own place in the world. You will ignite passion and a love of learning in your students. You will give students the keys to a better and more enriched life. And if you're lucky, you will literally change the world.

Teaching isn't for wimps. You have to decide whether the joys of teaching are really worth the nonsense we often have to put up with to be here. This is neither a political call to action nor a soothing chicken soup for the teacher's soul. Because I'm a realist and a pragmatist, this is something much more simple. Teaching has its challenges. But it also has its benefits. You have to decide whether the benefits make it worth dealing with the challenges.

If you decide to be here, be amazing. Don't settle for anything less. Some teachers are content to be mediocre. They have rationalized the fact that they don't reach every student every year and have learned to live with helping most children—just not all of them. They've become complacent, by choice or by circumstance. It's tragic, really. They no longer believe that they can become master teachers, so they talk themselves into being merely okay. Competent, even. Maybe they blame the kids, or perhaps they point to circumstances as their excuse. But the truth is, they've learned to settle. They don't believe that mastery is possible, so they stop reaching.

Don't you settle. Don't let anyone who has given up on their dreams of mastery rob you of yours. Mastery isn't easy, but it's possible if you reach for it. Not only is it possible, it's necessary—for your students, for their families, and for your own happiness. It will make the difference, all the difference, between merely teaching students how to decode and utilize text features and inspiring in them a lifelong love of reading and learning. It will make the difference between showing students how to add, subtract, multiply, and divide and helping them become effective problem solvers. It will make the difference between showing students how to conduct experiments and instilling in them a true wonder for the world and all that is in it. It will make the difference between requiring students to recite dates and facts, and helping them to understand their place in history and the connections between the past and their future. It will make the difference between teaching art, and music, computer science, and physical education and helping students build rich, interesting, meaningful lives. You don't have to settle. You can be a master teacher.

You can do this.

Chapter 1

- Do you have dreams about the kind of teacher you'll be? Do you think those dreams are more about your own vision of yourself (ego-driven) or more about the way you'll help your students?
- Are there some techniques or approaches preferred by your colleagues that just aren't working in your own practice? What other approaches could you try that might be more effective with your students and your teaching style?

Chapter 2

- Think of something you can do—every day—to provide a break from thinking about work and restore your soul. This could be as small a commitment as reading one page of a novel, or even walking once around your block to get fresh air and clear your head.

- Do you assign any homework that might not be benefit-ting your students, but feel that if you didn't assign it, you'd be a bad teacher? Think about what assignments you can trim down.
- Think about one passion you can pursue in your per-sonal life that will be interesting for your students to hear about. Taking a sailing course? Working on your poetry? Playing pickup softball?

Chapter 3

- What advice have you received from well-meaning col-leagues or friends that is simply not working with your own teaching practice?
- Prioritize your strategies. Identify *one* shift you can concentrate on making in the classroom.
- How can you show more vulnerability to your students?

Chapter 4

- Think about what you're teaching your class this week. *Why* are you teaching it?
- Look at your curriculum. What are your "need-to-knows," and what are your "nice-to-knows"?

Chapter 5

- Make a list of parents you're going to reach out to with *good* news in the next week. This could be as short as a two-sentence email.
- Do you find that your "bad news" conversations with parents often derail? If so, how can you restructure these conversations so they follow the four-step plan offered in Chapter 5 (Give them the news, along with your plan; Ask for input; Enlist help, and be specific; End with something good)?

Chapter 6

- Think about the last few classroom management problems you've encountered. Which were discipline problems? Which were motivation problems?
- Are you falling into the trap of acting like your students' peer? How can you slowly shift away from doing this into a more professional demeanor?
- Have you ever embarrassed a student? How could you have handled this situation differently to save the student embarrassment?

Chapter 7

- Are you failing any of your students? What strategies could you try to help these students?

- Have you beaten yourself up over a teaching mistake (or even catastrophe)? We all have. Think of ways to learn your lesson from this incident and move on.

Chapter 8

- What kind of support have you found most helpful in the past? Is there someone (a mentor or an administrator) who could provide this support for you now?
- Does your mentor feel comfortable telling you the truth about your teaching, warts and all? If not, what can you do to help make your mentor more comfortable in sharing that truth with you?
- From the last PD workshop you attended, what was one technique you heard about that you can apply to your own practice?

Chapter 9

- In what ways have you been more concerned about "looking good" than "being good"?
- What is your passion? What drove you to become an educator? Is your current role helping you fulfill that mission?
- Do you have aspirations for a promotion in the near future? Will that new job help you to fulfill your mission?

- What can you do to make professional connections outside your school?

Chapter 10

- Have you "borrowed a *why*"? Does this *why* truly fit with your own passion and mission?
- What is one of the messiest parts of being a teacher in your experience? What can you do to learn to accept the messiness?
- Are there any voices in your life—from friends, colleagues, or family members—making you think that maybe you can't do this? How can you overcome those voices and channel positive energy?